Poolology

Mastering the Art of Aiming

A Bookymonster Publication
Published 2017

Poolology - Mastering the Art of Aiming
ISBN 978-1-5323-5226-3
Softcover Edition

A few words concerning this 2nd edition of Poolology

When I first published this book I had no idea how the material would be received. Overall I was very optimistic, though one thought would occasionally come to mind: *With an abundance of pool books already available in the world, many of them top-notch, why would anyone choose to purchase mine?* Then it began to sell...one copy here, one there, two here, three there... From California to Florida, then Germany, Australia, Canada, etc...the book was selling!

The acceptance of Poolology throughout the pool world has been very gratifying, and the comments and opinions on the material have been encouraging, as well as eye-opening. Players all around the globe want to know more about the system. They want the details. How exactly does it work? How did you come up with it? What are the system limitations? Do you have more material? The questions and comments keep coming.

Due to such overwhelming feedback, I decided to update the book by adding material that had previously been edited out of the first edition prior to publication. The material was cut in an effort to produce a more user-friendly, simple product. This new edition of Poolology addresses many of the questions/issues related to the first edition.

It is important to note that I did not want the book to be a technical manual. Focusing on the technical aspects of aiming does not simplify the process. I wanted to present the Poolology aiming system in the simplest manner possible, without being too brain-numbing. I believe aiming should be approached from an artistic view point, not a technical one. After all, the subtitle of the book is, "Mastering the *Art* of Aiming", not "Mastering the *Geometry* of Aiming". With that said, there is some information that should've been included in the first edition. And so here we are, beginning this second edition of Poolology.

The material presented in this book is geared toward helping a player develop a natural feel for pocketing balls. If you want to be the type of player that just "sees the shots", which is how most professional pool players describe their aiming technique, you are in the right place. Just keep in mind that aiming systems aren't magic. They will not miraculously turn you into a pro-level player overnight. The road to becoming a great player requires more than just pocketing balls. You must pay attention to the many intricacies involved with all aspects of the game. I believe this book can get you there, but it will also require some attention and cooperation from *you*, the player.

Brian Crist

Poolology

Table of Contents

Introduction

Poolology is a book for pool players that wish to play better pool. The main focus of the book deals with aiming – shot making. So if you want to become a consistent shot maker, this book is for you.

Unlike conventional "old school" learning method, Poolology is quick to learn and simple to apply. Conventionally, learning to pocket pool balls involves shooting hundreds of practice shots, over and over. Eventually, through trial and error, you learn how to make most shots on the table. It is slow and monotonous work, requiring a certain level of dedication that the average pool player is simply unable or unwilling to give. As a result, a great number of pool players become stagnant in skill level, never reaching that next step, continually struggling for consistency.

Learning how to pocket balls should not be a struggle. It should not be tedious and boring work. It should be enjoyable. With Poolology you will quickly discover the simplicity of mastering every shot, and you'll have fun doing it because the results are immediate.

Since the main focus of Poolology deals with aiming, you should already be capable of holding a cue stick. In no way is this book intended to teach a beginner how to play pool. But if you can pocket three or four basic shots in a row before missing, and can use a little draw or follow without miscuing, then you'll have no problem applying the lessons here. Soon you'll be running more than just three or four balls…. You'll be running racks!

About Poolology

I began playing pool when I was sixteen. Like most young players, I had visions of becoming the next Willie Mosconi or Mike Sigel. To make a long story short, it didn't quite work out. Five-hour practice sessions when I was a teenager have dwindled down to thirty or forty minutes now, once a week, just enough to keep a slightly better than average stroke.

When I began writing this book, one question kept entering my head: *Who am I to write an instructional book on pool?* I'm not a top-caliber player, not a certified instructor or known figure in the world of pool and billiards. I'm not even the best player in my one-poolroom home town. I'm among the best, but wouldn't consider myself the best. I'd almost talked myself out of the book idea, then thought of all the lessons I'd learned over the years, from do-it-yourself automotive repairs to solving tricky calculus problems. I realized that the greatest lessons usually came from regular people like you and me, not from certified mechanics or mathematical geniuses.

Simply put, the best of the best are not always the best teachers. When a certain skill is mastered, whether it's throwing a football or knocking 2¼-inch balls into the pockets of a pool table, it should not be assumed that the art of *teaching* that skill to someone else is automatically mastered as well. Any well-known professional sports figure can write a book claiming to reveal his or her secrets and the book will sell. Aspiring young pool players are all too eager to purchase secrets of expert players. Unfortunately, after spilling out $29.99, $49.99, or whatever, they find no secrets. Instead, they find the same information found in every other book written by every other expert.

This is why the best instructional books are often written by relatively unknown players, people that have mastered the art of teaching rather than playing. And this isn't to say they aren't great players themselves, only that they are better teachers. With that said,

I wouldn't discourage anyone from buying any instructional book. I believe every book contains at least one lesson to be learned, one nugget that can be added to your bag of skills. Is it always worth the price of the book? Well, that's up to the individual player I suppose.

So what about Poolology? What does all of this have to do with me writing this book, other than the fact that I am an unknown? Like you, I just want to play better pool. I want to be a more consistent shot maker. I've been playing pool nearly thirty years, and, though I play great at times, I've never mastered the game (If mastering such a game is even possible!). Sometimes I feel unbeatable, breaking and running racks, making every shot, playing perfect position, and then other times I'll miss a shot that is so simple I feel like I should sell my cue and take up something less demanding, like power-napping or marshmallow roasting.

Fortunately, in my case, there are more good times than bad. Because of this my cue remains safe and not in danger of being traded for a good pillow or used as firewood. Other players are less fortunate, and I find myself wondering how they can continue playing the game if they aren't getting any better, if improvement seems hopeless.

I've players that continually struggle, never improving, while others shift gears, moving on up from one skill level to the next. I watch league players that can't run five balls in a row on an open table, even though they've been playing the game for more than a decade. Then I catch a player in dead stroke that doesn't miss a ball for three hours. Other than a certain degree of natural skill or hand-eye coordination, what separates these two types of players? Why does one player excel more quickly than another? Are some pool players simply not capable of improvement? I don't think so. I believe all players can improve if they're willing to learn, willing to become students of the game.

A few months ago I was in a pool hall in Atlanta, Georgia, practicing straight pool. I was on a good run to beat a personal record of 78 balls when I missed a simple cut shot down the rail. There were two players at the adjacent table, and when I missed that shot one of them asked how many balls I'd made. I said, "forty-four". And he asked, "How do you aim?" I thought about it, and then told him I didn't know. I'm sure he thought I was holding out on him, keeping some great pool secret to myself. But I really didn't know.

This incident is what put me on the path to writing this book. That question, *How do you aim?*, just wouldn't go away. I began asking other players (from very strong "A" players to average "C" players) how they go about aiming. I learned that every player aims in his or her own way, but no one could really explain it, other than to call it *instinct*. Like me, most players just feel where to aim. We aim toward a general spot that we think will send the object ball to the pocket, rather than to a specific point that we know will send the ball to the pocket. *Thinking*, however, is not the same as *knowing*.

I became determined to find a more dependable method of aiming. I wasted a few days on numerous aiming systems, which I won't bother listing here because none of them proved to be effective. I wanted a sure thing, an aiming system that would be simple, accurate, and effective.

Utilizing fractional ball hits and the various angles associated with pocketing balls, I've developed a system that easily provides an aim point for any given shot. Instead of aiming where you *think* you need to aim, you can now aim to where you *know* you need to aim. The difference is game-changing! From novice to advanced players, the information contained in this book will blow the doors wide open to pocketing balls with a higher degree of consistency. Welcome to Poolology.

Fundamentals

A good review of the basic fundamentals can never hurt anyone. In this section we'll take a brief look at the key elements needed to get the most out of this book. I'm referring to stance, grip, and stroke. Without having at least a basic understanding of these elements, your game will not improve. No system can replace basic fundamentals.

Stance

This is easy. Stand in manner that feels comfortable, not forced. Whatever feels natural for you will work just fine. Too many books try to teach people exactly where to put which leg or which foot, how much weight goes here or there, point this toe left and this one right, etc... The problem with this is that we are not robots. Unlike a spandex shooting glove, the stance is an individualized thing, not a one-size-fits-all.

Compare a great snooker player with a great nine ball player. The snooker player uses a more open, prone-position stance, while the nine ball player adopts the more traditional stance; one leg forward and slightly bent, the back leg vertically aligned with the shooting arm. By comparison, both players are great shot makers, yet their stances are not the same.

Your stance should be *your* stance, not an imitation of someone else's. However, if imitating another player's stance feels right for you, then by all means do it! The main purpose of the stance is to provide your body with a comfortable shooting position, a position that won't feel forced, won't feel like a workout for your legs or the rest of your body. It's a natural process that your body usually figures out on its own. No book can teach you that. Basically, do what feels best, and keep doing it until you don't have to think about it anymore.

If you can't seem to find a stance that feels comfortable, and you try and try but still can't settle into a good stance, then you're probably not meant to be a pool player. Try darts or bowling.

Grip

Do not use a white-knuckle death grip. Remember that it's the cue stick (not your fist) that strikes the cue ball. Hold the butt/handle of the cue lightly, primarily between your thumb and forefinger. The remaining fingers should just barely touch the grip, if they touch it at all. This is the most common grip. You may find that your grip differs from this, and that's fine if it does, as long as the cue moves freely with a smooth stroke – no up or down or sideways glitches.

Stroke

Not enough can be said about the importance of a good stroke. The stroke should be smooth and straight. Do not flick or twist your wrist at the end of the stroke when applying english or draw. This results in nothing special, other than inconsistency, which is not good. Spin is applied by using a good follow through, not by twisting your stick.

A great practice routine for developing a true stroke is to align your bridge hand over the top of the cushion, right above the point where the wood on the rail meets the cloth. Stroke along that line and watch your shaft in comparison. It should not sway left or right.

Another good practice technique is to lay an empty soda bottle down on the table, form a bridge about 8 to 10 inches from the mouth of the bottle and stroke the cue in and out of the bottle. If you can do this without ever touching the lip/rim of the bottle then your stroke is probably fine. The more accurate you stroke the cue stick the more consistent you'll be at aiming and striking the cueball. If your stroke is faulty, you'll always have problems aiming certain shots.

Of course, we can't talk about stroke without mentioning the bridge and the follow through. Typically, the standard bridge is about 8 to 10 inches. This is the distance from your bridge hand to the cueball. It really depends on what feels natural to you. If you have a perfect stroke, it really won't make a difference whether or not you play with a short bridge or a super-long bridge. But if you have any flaws or inconsistencies in your stroke, you should play with a shorter bridge until the flaws can be worked out.

The more cue stick you have dangling out beyond your bridge hand, the more amplified the flaws become. To prove this point, try breaking the balls with your bridge hand closer to the cueball, a very short bridge of about four or five inches. You'll notice a more solid, consistent break. The reason why is because when we break we tend to use more power, which affects accuracy when striking the cue ball. Shortening the bridge de-amplifies this effect, resulting in a more accurate shot.

The final part of the stroke is the follow-though. It is most important! With each shot allow your cue stick to naturally follow straight through the cue ball to a point several inches beyond where the cue ball was resting. Your exact follow-through could be anywhere from four to eight inches depending on your stroke. Never stop your cue from finishing the entire stroke, except on those shots in which you must stop the cue to avoid a double-kiss or hitting another ball. Incorporating a good follow through will tremendously improve your shot making skills and your position play.

Mentality – Thinking and Knowing

If you want to start pocketing more balls, you need to develop a good relationship between thinking and knowing. In life, we *think* of what to do and then we execute what we *know*. It's that simple. Problems occur when we attempt to execute something that we don't exactly know how to execute. In pool, this leads to missed shots, poor safeties, and overall bad play.

In order to establish a dependable relationship between thinking and knowing, you must acknowledge your current limitations. Every pool player has limitations. Realizing and accepting these limitations will make you a better player.

I remember years ago, gambling with an old guy we called "Sawdust", I'd try a world-beater shot and sellout the game. He'd say, "You gotta know your limitations, kid." It took years for me to realize that he was right. I thought I was invincible, and would shoot at everything, like a kid in a candy store grabbing at every piece of candy he sees, not understanding that some of the candy was simply out of reach. I know better now.

Reserve the out-of-reach shots for practice, not tournament matches or gambling sessions. Eventually those shots will become part of your normal game. Until then, keep them filed away as limitations, as personal weaknesses. And remember the old saying: *Knowing your own weaknesses is more of an advantage than knowing those of your opponent.*

Thinking and knowing require control. When you are at the table *you* are in control. You are the decision maker. This is why it is important to have a realistic understanding of what you are capable of doing. Your opponent sits and waits, watching, wondering what you're going to do next. He has no control at the moment. You are in control, and this is when thinking and knowing become crucial.

Do all of your thinking while standing up. Never think while you're down over a shot. Imagine the entire room split into two planes, each parallel to the floor. The upper plane, from your chest to the ceiling, is where you do all of your thinking and planning. The lower plane, from your chest to the floor, which includes the table, is where you execute what you know.

There are always distractions in the upper plane, such as music, people talking, people moving about, etc... **Acknowledge all distractions**. You will never be able to do away with distractions, but giving them a second or two of your attention in the upper plane will help keep them from polluting your head in the lower plane.

When you are in the lower plane, down on the shot, you are in execution/performance mode. Do not shoot the shot if you become distracted or if something doesn't feel right. Stand up and deal with it right away in the upper plane. Only move from the upper plane to the lower plane when you feel certain that the shot you intend to execute is reasonably within your current limitations. "Reasonably" means you have at least a 75-80% chance of pulling it off, and won't sellout the game if you don't pull it off. The shot could be as simple as a little bump-safety if that's all you feel comfortable doing. *You* are in control.

Above all, remain positive. Remaining positive will keep you feeling comfortable, which in turn will build confidence. When a shot doesn't turn out well, move on and leave it in the past. You made a mistake. It's that simple. We all make mistakes. Don't blame it on bad luck caused by mysterious "Pool Gods" that have it out for you. The fact is, there are good rolls and bad rolls, and most of the time the bad rolls are due to carelessness on our part. Sometimes the rolls are due to conditions we have no control over. When you get a good roll, don't say to yourself that you got lucky. Say you made that happen because that's how good you are. When you get a bad roll, don't blame luck or imaginary gods. Learn from it. Maybe there's a way you could've avoided that entire situation. Give it about five seconds of analysis and move on.

17

As soon as you quit making excuses for your mistakes you'll find yourself improving as a player. It's all about how you control the relationship between thinking and knowing. When a shot comes up that requires a little guess work, a little roll to go your way, focus on what you *want* to happen, not on what you are afraid *might* happen.

Remember: *The upper plane is for thinking, the lower plane is for execution. Incorporate this thought process into your game and you'll find yourself winning more often.*

Mastering the Art of Aiming

It's been said that there are no shortcuts or secrets to pocketing balls, other than countless hours of practice, followed by more and more practice. This is no longer true. Utilizing the fractional-ball aiming technique presented in this book, you can rapidly improve your shot making skills in record time. Fractional-ball aiming is not a new concept, but you need to understand the basics of it in order to fully comprehend what Poolology can do for you.

Fractional ball aiming refers to a method where the cut angle of any given shot corresponds to a specific fractional hit between the cue ball and the object ball. For starters, we are going to focus on the four basic fractional hits shown below, known as the "quarters". The aim points used to obtain these fractional hits are also shown, where the cue ball is white and object ball is black.

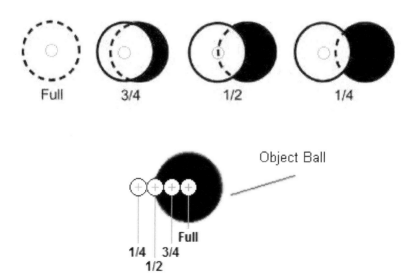

Diagram 1 - Basic Fractional Aim Points

Our goal is to master these four basic fractional aim points. By shooting through the center of the cue ball to a matching fractional aim point located on or near the object ball, the corresponding fractional hit is achieved. For example, shooting the center of the cue ball to the 3/4 aim point will produce a 3/4 fractional ball hit, and aiming at the 1/2 aim point will produce a 1/2 ball hit, and so on.

Naturally, there will be shots that fall between the basic aim points, like a shot that needs to be hit a bit thicker (more full) than a 1/2 ball hit, but not as thick as a 3/4 ball hit. The Poolology aiming system will provide the appropriate aim point for shots between straight-in and a 1/8 ball hit, using the basic quarter aim points above, as well as *in-between* aim points in eighth intervals. Refer to the section titled, "In-between Basic Aim Points". For cut shots thinner than a 1/8 fractional aim, a player must develop his or her own feel in order to achieve consistency.

In the next few pages we'll be taking a closer look at each of these basic fractional hits. Note that each shot diagram (except for the full ball hit) provides two views of the shot – an overhead view, where the cue stick is lined directly for the aim point, and an eclipse/overlap view as seen from behind the cue ball as it collides with the object ball. In the overlap view you'll notice a small circle. This circle represents the aim point on the object ball. The tip of your cue stick should be lined straight through the center of the cue ball to this exact circular aim point for each fractional hit.

Full-ball

A full ball hit is very basic. Note that each of the following diagrams depicts an overhead view of the shot. A full ball hit, as shown below, produces no cut angle. It is center-to-center, a straight-in shot. Simple enough.

Diagram 2 - Straight Shot

Not much can go wrong here as long as long we don't apply too much side spin on the cue ball. Straight-in shots are generally not complicated. Side spin (english) causes the cue ball to squirt, which alters the point of contact between the cue ball and object ball. It can also cause object ball throw, which changes the natural path of the object ball upon impact. The effects of english and how to compensate for it are covered in the section titled, "Applying English".

In addition to english, another factor that affects aiming on straight-in shots is the distance between the cue ball and object ball. Distance affects aiming accuracy. A good stroke is needed to consistently pocket long, straight-in shots. In other words, you need to be consistent at hitting the spot you are aiming at, whether it's six inches away or six feet.

Three-quarter-ball

A 3/4 ball hit is the result of aiming halfway between the center and the edge of the object ball, which means 3/4 of the cue ball will **overlap** with 3/4 of the object ball upon impact. Since 3/4 will overlap, this leaves 1/4 of the cue ball (25%) hanging outside the edge of the object ball. We'll call this 1/4 the overhang. Remember not to concern yourself with percentages or fractions. Just knowing how to hit the aim point is enough for now.

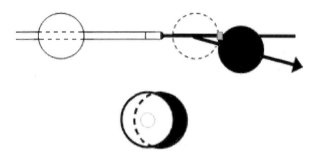

Diagram 3 - 3/4 Ball Hit/Aim Point

The 3/4 ball hit sends the object ball away at a slight angle from the aim line (about 15 degrees). We are not concerned with the exact angle. All we need to know is where to aim in order to shoot the shot. Aim through the center of the cue ball to a point exactly halfway between the center and the edge of the object ball, as shown above.

Practice these fractional hits by striking the cue ball about half a tip above center with medium speed (not hard, not soft). If the cue ball slides into the object ball, a stun shot, the object ball will be thrown off angle by a few degrees, possibly resulting in a missed shot. If english is used, the cue ball will squirt sideways a little and will not contact the object ball at the desired angle. We will study the effects of english in the next chapter. It is best to initially practice these aim points with no english until you become familiar and accurate with each fractional shot.

Half-ball

For a 1/2 ball hit we aim our cue tip to split the outer edge of the object ball. This is the simplest cut shot to achieve because we have a well-defined aim point – the edge of the object ball. Since half of the cue ball (50%) will be outside the edge of the object ball on this shot, our **overlap** is 1/2 a ball. This shot produces a cut angle of approximately 30 degrees, minus a couple of degrees due to the collision-induced throw that occurs naturally at this angle.

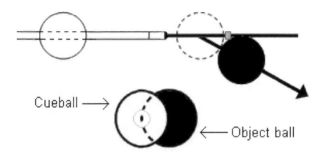

Cueball ⟶

⟵ Object ball

Diagram 4 - 1/2 Ball Hit/Aim Point

The 1/2 ball hit is the most important of our four basic fractional hits. It is by far the most valuable shot on the pool table. Later in this chapter, when the aiming system diagrams are revealed, you will learn how *every* cut shot can be gauged simply by visualizing the 1/2 ball shot.

Another tip about 1/2 ball hits is that both balls leave the collision point at nearly equal speeds, which means they also travel equal distances from each other. This is great to know when playing a safety shot or fine-tuning position play for the next shot.

Quarter-ball

The aim point for a 1/4 ball shot is accomplished by aiming at a point outside the object ball that would cause the side of our cue shaft to be about 1/4 of an inch from the edge of the object ball, if the shaft could reach that far on the follow through stroke. It also depends on the diameter of your shaft. The exact aim point is 9/16 of inch from the edge of the object ball. So if you aim the center of your cue tip to that exact spot, the edge of your shaft would be about 1/4 to 3/10 of an inch from the edge of the ball. Using your cue tip/shaft is a good way to visualize the correct aim.

This hit causes 1/4 of the cue ball (25%) to **overlap** the object ball during impact, while 75% (or 3/4) of the cue ball overhangs the edge of the object ball. The shot angle is about 48 degrees. Factoring in throw, depending on shot speed, the angle is closer to 45 degrees.

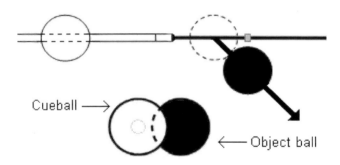

Diagram 5 - 1/4 Ball Hit/Aim Point

Of our basic fractional hits, the quarter ball is the toughest. Be sure to use your cue tip/shaft to assist you with locating the aim point. This cut is especially difficult from a distance, so weigh your options carefully. A safety is often the best choice, rather than trying a thin cut on an object ball more than 6 feet away from the cue ball.

On a "bar box" table the pockets are more forgiving and many shots can be made simply by using the basic aim points. If it's close to a half ball shot, then a half ball aim will probably work. But not all tables are this easy. You'll always have in-between shots, and on the bigger tables, or tables with tighter pockets, you'll definitely need to use more than these basic aim points. If the shot requires a slight cut, but not quite 3/4, then you'll use a 7/8 aim.

Throughout this book we will be using these basic quarter aim points, as well as in-between aim points as shown on the following page.

In-Between Basic Aim Points

Each fractional hit in this diagram shows where the tip of your cue stick should be aimed (the gray circle) in order to achieve the desired fractional hit.

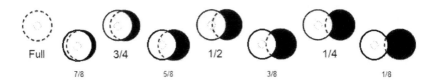

Be sure to use your cue tip/shaft to help visualize the various aim points. For instance, a 5/8 hit requires your cue shaft (at the tip) to be flush inside the edge of the object ball, halfway between a 1/2 ball aim and a 3/4 ball aim. For a 3/8 hit the shaft would be flush against the outside edge of the object ball. The image below should provide a better understanding of the the exact location for each in-between aim point. Study it and practice hitting these aim points.

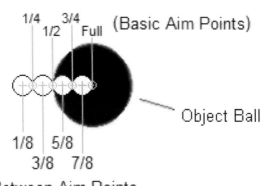

In-Between Aim Points

Well, that's it for the basic fractional hits. Are you ready to start putting all of this fractional aiming business to work? The following

26

pages contain the most accurate aiming system ever developed for playing pool. Study the diagrams carefully.   Instead of thinking about fractions, think in terms of cue ball overlap/overhang. **The overlap always represents the fractional hit being used.**

Do not be overwhelmed by the main diagram on the next page, titled *Corner Pocket Aiming Zones*. It merely shows all three corner pocket zones at once. In the examples that follow, we will break each zone down individually and you'll see that it's not as complicated as it may initially appear.

Corner Pocket Aiming Zones

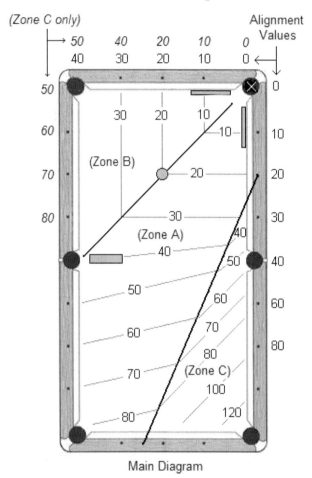

Main Diagram

Each zone has its own object ball position lines, like yard lines on a football field. These lines determine the object ball's **position value** on the table. The numbers alongside the diamond markers provide an **alignment value** for the shot. This value is found by visualizing the *natural line* from the center of the cue ball through the center of the object ball, straight through to the rail. We'll use the simple ratio between these two values to determine fractional hits for cut shots.

28

NOTE: There are some areas where the system is less accurate, comprising about 1% of the table's playing surface. These areas are grayed-out in the above diagram and described as follows:

> ➢ The circle at the 20/20 intersection between Zones A and B is slightly outside of the system's parameters (see the original concept image in the "How it All Works" section at the back of the book). The rectangle area in Zone A on the 40 position line is also outside of the parameters. Object balls in these areas should be shot using **one eighth fractional aim point THICKER** than the system indicates. (If the system calls for a 1/4 shot, use a 3/8 instead.)

> ➢ Object balls in the thin rectangle areas near the targeted corner pocket (frozen or closer than half an inch from the cushion) should be hit **one quarter fractional aim point THINNER** than the system indicates. (From this particular approach angle the cushion interferes with the shot line. If the system indicates a 1/2 ball shot, we should aim for the 1/4 aim point instead.)

Zone A

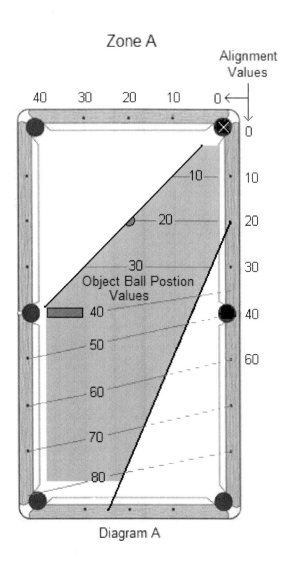

Diagram A

The largest percentage of shots takes place in Zone A, the shaded area above. If we are shooting toward the upper right-hand pocket, and the object ball is located anywhere in the shaded area, we will use the object ball position values in Zone A to determine our aim point. If we were shooting to any other corner pocket, we would flip this

30

diagram so that it corresponds to that particular pocket.

It is important to note that the location of the object ball is what determines which zone to use for any particular shot. Cue ball location is irrelevant.

An object ball resting on 30 in Zone A has a position value of 30. Anywhere along the 30 line would be considered an **object ball position** of 30. Next we find the **alignment value** of the shot by following the natural line from the center of the cue ball through the center of the object ball, then straight on through to an alignment value on the long or short rail. The ratio between the alignment value and the object ball position value provides us with the ***overhang***, the exact fraction of the cue ball that needs to be outside the edge of the object ball in order to make the shot. Knowing how much of the cue ball needs to be *overhanging* the object ball tells us how much must ***overlap***. If 1/4 is overhanging, then 3/4 must overlap.

The OVERLAP always indicates the fractional aim point needed to pocket the ball.

We'll begin with some standard 1/2 ball shots. In this diagram the **object ball position** has a value of **40**. The natural line points to an **alignment value** of **20** on the side rail. The ratio between 20 and 40 is **1/2**, which means half of the cue ball must overhang (be outside of) the edge of the object ball upon impact. The other half must **overlap** the object ball, making this a half-ball hit. Our aim line should be directed at the **1/2** ball aim point.

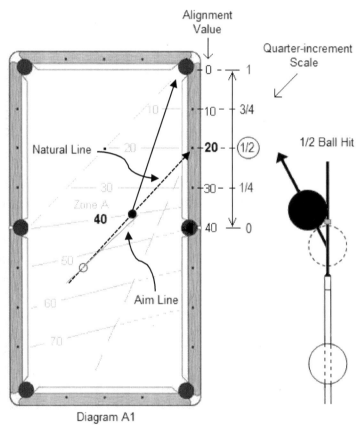

Diagram A1

The "Quarter-increment scale" along the side rail is another way to visualize the shot. This scale directly shows the *overlap* fraction of the shot, or better yet, the fractional aim point needed to make the shot. Visualize a scale as shown in this diagram, with 0 at an alignment value equal to the object ball position value, and 1 at the targeted pocket. Now locate the halfway point and the quarter increments along the rail. The diamonds can assist you with this. The natural line, in addition to giving us the alignment value, will now be pointing directly at the required fractional aim point on our quarter-increment scale, which for this particular shot is **1/2**.

Here is another half-ball shot in Zone A. The **object ball position** is **20**. The natural line (from the center of the cueball through the center of the object ball) leads to an **alignment value** of **10** on the side rail, a ratio of 1/2. Half of the cue ball will overhang the object ball while the other half overlaps it. A 1/2 ball hit will send this object ball into the corner pocket. For visualization practice, note how the natural line points to the "1/2" mark on our added quarter-increment scale.

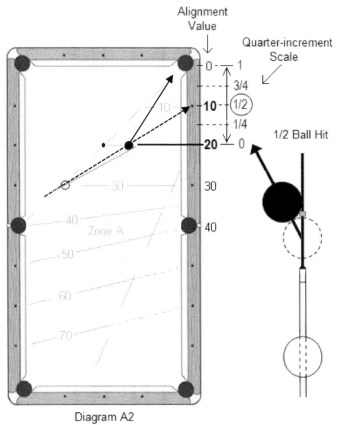

Diagram A2

Remember that the ratio between the alignment value and the object ball position reflects the *overhang* amount. This is the fraction of the cue call that needs to be outside the edge of the object ball when the two balls collide. The **overlap** is the fraction of the cue ball that actual collides with the object ball. A 1/2 ball hit produces 50% overhang and 50% overlap. A straight in shot has no overhang because the cue ball overlaps the object ball 100%.

You can improve your visualization skills by viewing every cut shot in terms of cue ball *overhang* and *overlap*. **And keep in mind that the overlap always indicates the fractional hit needed to pocket the object ball.**

Be sure to use the shaft of your cue stick as an aide to help visualize and aim the shot. You already know where the center of the cue ball should be headed in order to achieve a specific fractional shot. It should be headed toward the aim point, so your cue stick should be stroked along the exact line (the aim line) leading to that point. That's the solution for every shot, and we get there by simply comparing two values – the natural alignment value (where the object ball would hit if we were to shoot the cue ball straight into it, center-to-center), and the object ball position value on the table.

In this example, even though the natural line points toward the side rail, the distance between the object ball and the pocket makes it difficult to visualize a quarter-increment scale. However, we can easily determine that this is a half-ball shot. The object ball position is around **52**. The alignment value lands very close to **26**, which is half. So a **1/2** ball fractional hit will send this object ball into the far corner pocket with no trouble.

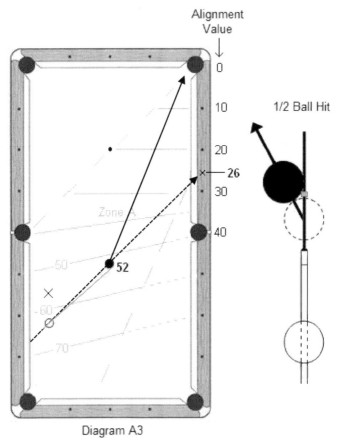

Diagram A3

If we kept the object ball at 52 and moved the cue ball to the "X" mark, our new alignment value would be around 36 instead of 26, making this shot closer to a 1/4 aim. (You could use a calculator and determine that an overhang of 36/52 is around 70%. So if 70% of the cue ball would need to be outside the edge of the object ball on impact, 30% would have to overlap it, which is slightly thicker than a 1/4 ball aim, but not so thick that a 1/4 aim would not work.)

Now drop the calculator and forget the math. Simply think like this: Our object ball is at a position of 52; half of 52 is 26, and half of 26 is 13. This gives us the quarter-increment values for our basic aim points, which are increments of 13 for this particular object ball position. Knowing this, we can now compare our alignment value with our known quarter-increment values to determine which aim point to use.

With an object ball position of 52, an alignment value of **26** would be a 1/2 ball shot. One increment more (26+13=**39**) would be a 1/4 ball shot. Our alignment value with the cue ball at position "X" would be around 36, which is thinner than a 1/2 aim but thicker than a 1/4 aim. The in-between aim point between a 1/2 and a 1/4 is the 3/8 aim point. For this shot, an alignment value near 32 or 33 would indicate a 3/8 aim (half way between 26 and 39). A value of 36 would actually be aiming between a 3/8 and a 1/4 aim point. **It is always better to slightly overcut a ball than hit it too full.** The reason involves collision-induced throw, which thickens most cut shots up a bit. So choosing the 1/4 aim point would be the smarter option here.

With this example (object ball at 52, alignment value of 36) you could even fine tune your aim if you have the skill to do so. Poolology sticks with using aim points as fine as an eighth of a ball. This works for any shot within 4 or 5 diamonds from the pocket. Due to most pool table pockets being at least twice as wide as object balls, we have room for play, a margin of error, and we do not have to calculate exact percentages or fractions. At longer distances, on the other hand, our margin of error begins to shrink and more accuracy is needed.

When an object ball is very far away from the pocket, let's say 6 to 8 diamonds, nothing says you can't fine tune your aim by aiming a sixteenth thinner or thicker instead of going with the nearest eighth of a ball aim point. This is where you begin to develop a feel for certain shots. Odds are, unless you're playing on a tight table with 4½-inch or tighter pockets, you'll have no trouble pocketing balls using the basic quarter aim points and the in-between eighth aim points. Table experience will help you determine your most accurate options and when fine-tuning may be needed.

Using the 1/2 Ball Alignment Value to Gauge all Cut Shots

Recognizing when a shot is thinner or thicker than a half-ball will quickly help you develop better aiming skills. After all, the four basic aim points are just that...*basic*. Certain shots will inevitably fall between these basic aim points, like a 3/8 or a 5/8 shot (Refer to the "In-between Basic Aim Points" section). The quickest way to narrow any shot down to an exact aim point is to break it into quarter increments, like so:

Take the object ball position value and divide it in half. This is what your alignment value would have to be in order for the shot to be a 1/2 ball hit. For example, let's use an object ball position value of 30. Half of 30 is 15. If the alignment value of the shot is greater than 15, you will need to aim outside the edge of the cue ball for a thinner hit. If the alignment value is lower than 15, you'll have to aim for a thicker hit. How much thinner? How much thicker? Well, we can go one more step...

Divide 15 in half, which we'll call 8 (remember, we don't have to be exact). It's that simple! We have just scaled a shot down into quarter increments. We now know that we can use increments of 8 to determine the proper aim point for any particular shot that has an object ball position value of 30.

Next, we simply compare the alignment value of the shot to our quarter-increment values. With an object ball position of **30**, we know an alignment of value of **0** would be a full ball shot (straight in), **8** would be a 3/4 ball shot, **15** a 1/2 ball shot, and **23** a 1/4 ball shot. If the alignment value is equal (within a digit or two) to one of our basic quarter increment values, we aim for that corresponding fractional aim point. If the alignment value falls between two of our basic quarter increments, our aim point would be in-between those two specific aim points.

39

Let's say our object ball is positioned on 30 and we have an alignment value of 17. That might be close enough to our 1/2 ball aim point (alignment value of 15) to call it a 1/2 ball shot. This works fine as long as the object ball is within a few feet of the pocket. Remember, the farther away the ball is from the pocket, the more accurate we need to be when choosing the correct aim point. The more you practice breaking shots down into quarter increments (based on the object ball position value), the more proficient you'll become at recognizing the proper aim points and fine tuning them as needed.

It is important to remember that the system accurately determines aim points as thin as a 1/8 fractional shot. **Any time the alignment value is equal to or greater than the object ball position value, the shot requires a hit thinner than a 1/8 aim.**

This shot has an **object ball position** of about **32**. Notice the Zone A position lines/values are not shown. You must learn to visualize the position values as shown in previous examples. In this shot, the natural line points toward the end rail at an **alignment value** around **16**. Since 16 is 1/2 of 32, a standard **1/2** ball hit pockets the ball in the upper right-hand corner.

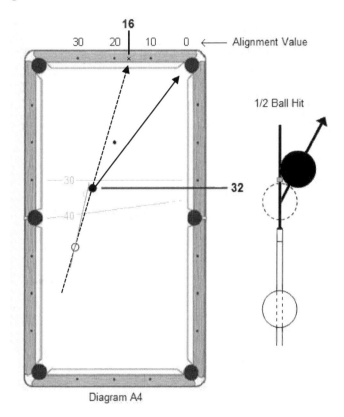

Diagram A4

Note: If we wanted to back-cut this ball into the left corner pocket, we would have to flip our zone diagram around to target that specific pocket. In that case, our alignment values on the end rail would start with zero at the left corner pocket instead of the right, making our alignment value a 24 instead of 16. The object ball position would still

41

be in Zone A at a position near 32, which would give us an overhang of 24/32, which is 3/4. That would leave an overlap of 1/4, making it a 1/4 ball shot to the left. Our aim point would be just outside the right edge of the object ball at the 1/4 ball aim point. Breaking this object ball position down into basic quarter increments tells us the quarter aim points are in increments of 8. So an alignment of 8 would be a 3/4 ball shot, 16 would be a 1/2 ball shot, and 24 would be a 1/4 ball shot. We'll be looking at 1/4 ball shots very soon.

Here is a back-cut with an object ball position of **40**. The natural line points to an alignment value of **20** on the end rail. A simple **1/2** ball hit on the right edge of the object ball will send it into the left corner pocket like a champ.

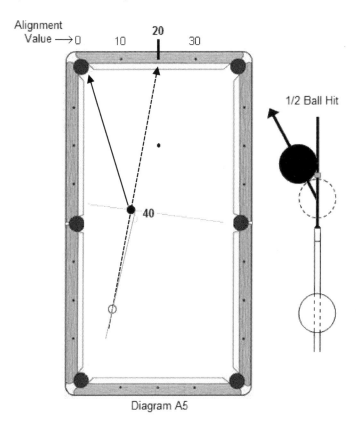

Diagram A5

This shot can also be made in the right corner pocket with a 1/2 ball hit to the *left* edge of the object ball. If we flip Zone A toward the right corner pocket, our object ball position value would be 38. The alignment value would still be 20. This would make it a touch thinner than a half-ball shot, but a 1/2 ball aim would still hit the pocket.

Anytime the object ball position is near 40, and the alignment value is near 20 on the end rail, the object ball can be made in either corner pocket with a 1/2 ball hit.

It's now time to move on to the 1/4 ball fractional shots. The aim point for a 1/4 ball hit is 9/16 of an inch from the outer most surface/edge of the object ball. The side of your cue shaft, if your stroke could carry the shaft all the way to the aim point, would be about 1/4 of an inch to 3/10 of an inch away from the edge of the object ball. Using the side of your shaft for a reference can be very useful and convenient for many of these aim points.

Here we have a ball in Zone A at a position of **20**. The natural line points to an alignment value of **15**. Since 15 is 3/4 of 20, our overhang is 3/4, leaving 1/4 of the cue ball to overlap the object ball upon impact. This is a **1/4** ball shot.

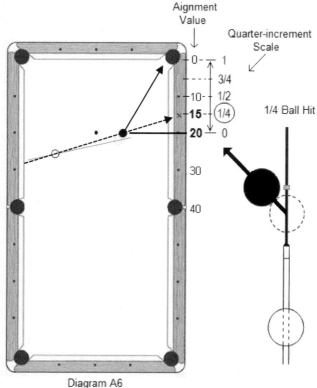

Diagram A6

If you can't visualize a quarter-increment scale along the rail, simply calculate the quarter increments in your head by dividing the object ball position in half twice (half of 20 is 10, and half of 10 is **5**). Our quarter aim points are in increments of 5. An alignment of **0** would be straight in, **5** would be a 3/4 shot, **10** would be a 1/2, and **15** a 1/4.

The next shot requires a little tweaking. The object ball is on that 20/20 intersection between Zones A and B (the spot) where the system is not quite asaccurate.

With an object ball position of 20 and an alignment value of 15, the numbers show that 3/4 of the cue ball must overhang the object ball at impact, leaving 1/4 to overlap. This indicates a 1/4 ball aim point should be used. However, as mentioned earlier, this spot falls within that 1% of the table surface where the math just isn't dead on. Shooting this shot with a 1/4 aim will overcut the ball.

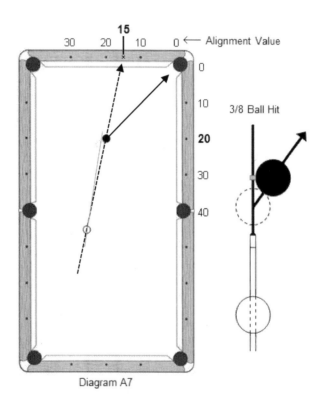

Diagram A7

We must compensate our aim by aiming **one eighth fractional aim point thicker.** Instead of aiming for a 1/4, we'll aim for a **3/8**. (Refer to "In-between Basic Aim Points")

Remember: *Any time the object ball is on the foot spot (or head spot if the shot's on that end of the table) you compensate your aim to hit one eighth thicker than the systemindicates.*

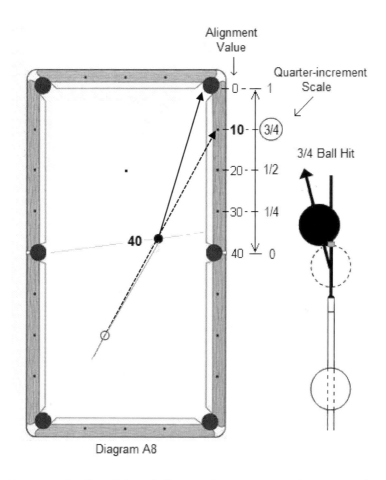

Diagram A8

In this example the object ball is in Zone A at position **40**. The natural line leads to an alignment value of **10**. This ratio (10/40) equates to an overhang of 1/4, leaving us an overlap of 3/4, which means a **3/4** ball hit will send the object ball into the pocket. Our basic aim points in this example (with an object ball position of 40) are in quarter increments of 10, which we determined by dividing 40 in half, giving us 20, then half of 20 gives us 10.)

Looking back at the previous shot, what if our alignment value were 15 instead of 10? We've already determined that our basic aim points for this shot (object ball position of 40) are in quarter increments of 10. So an alignment of 0 is straight in, 10 is a 3/4 ball shot, 20 a 1/2 ball shot, and 30 a 1/4 ball shot. An alignment value of 15 would put the shot between a 3/4 ball aim and a 1/2 ball aim, which is a **5/8** fractional hit.

Practice shooting these shots with no english, striking the cue ball just above center with a good follow through. You must be proficient at recognizing and hitting the appropriate aim point. English can alter the shot quite a bit. The main focus for now is to become consistent at hitting the appropriate aim points. English comes later.

Our final example in Zone A is a back-cut to the right corner pocket. Once again, the object ball is positioned on **40**. The natural line points to an alignment value of **10** on the end rail, indicating that 1/4 (25% overhang) of the cue ball must be outside the edge of the object ball upon impact. This means a 3/4 overlap is needed, and so we aim for a **3/4** ball hit.

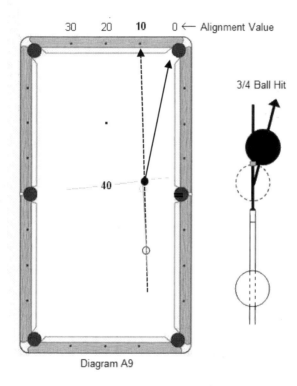

Diagram A9

You should memorize the Zone A diagram (Diagram A at the beginning of this section). Keep in mind that from 0 to 30 the object ball position values coincide with the alignment values along the side rail, like yard lines on a football field. Beyond 30, the position values shift a bit.

49

Practice the example shots and master the skill it takes to recognize and hit each fractional aim point. You should also setup your own practice shots within Zone A to further sharpen your zone visualization.

We're going to look at Zone B next, the second most common shot zone. As with Zone A, the same principles apply here. We will use object ball positions and alignment values to determine the proper overhangs/overlaps needed to pocket balls at various angles.

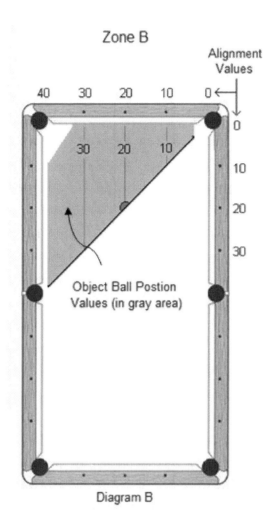

Diagram B

Zone B is the shaded area in Diagram B above. If we are shooting toward the top right-hand pocket, and the object ball is anywhere in this area, we will use the object ball position values for Zone B. (If we were shooting toward the upper left pocket, the shaded area and alignment scales would be flipped around, starting with zero from that corner.)

Zone B is very easy to recognize. Notice how the zone's boundary stretches diagonally from the targeted corner pocket to the opposite side pocket. Any ball between the end rail and this boundary line is in Zone B. Object ball position values coincide with the diamonds on the end rail, unlike Zone A where the object ball positions primarily coincide with the long rail diamonds. Alignment values can be located on either the end rail or the side rail, depending on the shot. In the next example, we'll look at a shot in Zone B where the alignment value is found on the end rail.

Remember, the position of the object ball is all that matters when determining which zone applies for any particular shot. The **position value** of an object ball in Zone B is determined by the position value lines originating from the end rail diamonds as shown above. The natural line is always from the center of the cue ball through the center of the object ball, all the way to the side or end rail, depending on the shot. It provides us with the **alignment value** of the shot.

Now let's look at some Zone B cut shots...

This object ball is at a position of **20** in Zone B. The natural line (from the center of the cue ball through the center of the object ball) points to an alignment value of **10** on the side rail. 10 is 1/2 of 20, indicating an overhang of half a ball, which leaves us an overlap of half a ball. Remember the overlap is equivalent to the aim point, so this is a **1/2** ball shot.

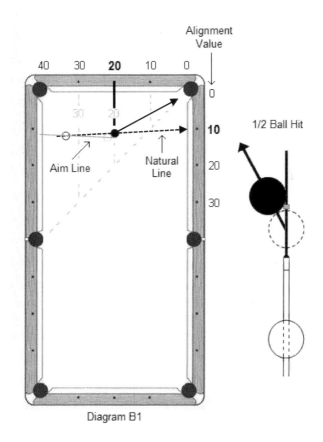

Diagram B1

When shooting this shot be sure to use rolling cue ball speed. If you hit the shot firm, a stun shot, there's a good chance the cue ball will scratch in the side pocket. The 90 degree angle looks fairly close here. Either shoot with a medium or soft rolling cue ball or use some back spin (draw) to pull the cue ball beyond that side pocket.

53

Here the object ball is positioned near **28** in Zone B. The natural line points to an alignment value of **20** on the end rail. We don't need to pull out our calculators to figure this shot out. Sure, to be exact, we could divide 20 by 28 and get an overhang of 71%, which would leave us an overlap of 29%, a touch thicker than a 1/4 ball shot. But instead of clouding our heads with fractions and calculations, we can simply break this shot down into basic quarter increments.

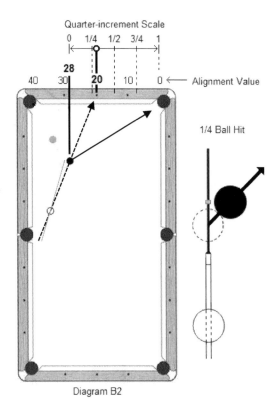

Diagram B2

For this shot we break it down by dividing 28 in half to get 14. If our alignment value were 14 this would be a 1/2 ball shot. But we are lined for 20, much thinner than a 1/2 ball shot. Taking it one step further, we divide 14 in half and get 7. This is our basic quarter-increment value. If a 1/2 ball shot is 14, then a 1/4 ball shot would be one increment greater than 14, or 14+7, which is **21**. With an alignment value of 20 (and the object within 3 feet of the pocket) we can easily make the shot with a **1/4** ball aim.

Our final Zone B example shows a standard **1/2** ball shot from cue ball "A". The object ball position is **20** and the natural line points to an alignment value of **10** on the end rail. From cue ball "B" this would be a 1/4 ball shot, as the natural line from that point would lead to an alignment value of 15.

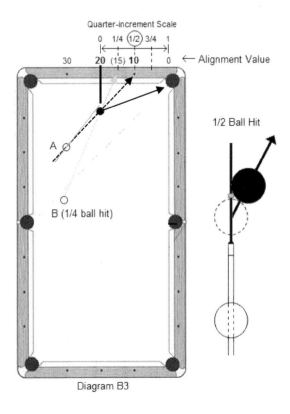

Diagram B3

Practice these examples, and then setup your own shots from various object ball positions within Zone B. Remember that it's the location of the object ball that determines the zone for each shot. The location of the cue ball is irrelevant, other than providing a cut angle for the shot.

56

Zone C

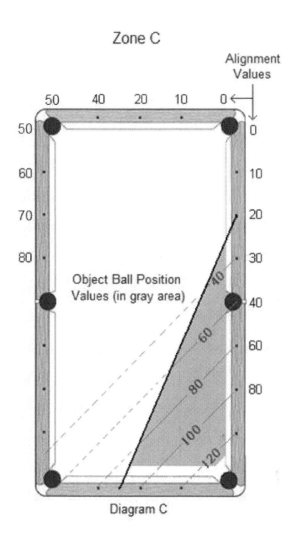

Diagram C

The last zone for corner pocket aiming is Zone C. It is a bit trickier than Zones A and B, but the aiming method is the same. We will use **object ball positions** and **alignment values** to determine our fractional ball aim points. Object ball position values are indicated in the shaded area (between 40 and 120).

57

Notice how the position value lines run diagonally from the end rail diamonds to the side rail diamonds. By standing at the end rail, and sighting diagonally over the object ball (parallel to the Zone C position lines), an accurate **object ball position** value can be determined. The **alignment value** is found by following the natural line to the values indicated on the side rails or end rail. Unlike Zones A and B, the alignment values do not coincide with the object ball position values, so do not confuse or mix the two. You should study this diagram thoroughly. Memorize it.

The next few pages contain various Zone C examples. We'll look a mix of 3/4, 1/2, and 1/4 ball shots. You should practice these shots with no english. We will bring english into play soon enough.

What makes Zone C tricky is the fact that the pocket is farther away from the object ball. The angle between the object ball and the pocket looks different due to added distance, and due to the long rail interfering with the visual perception of the shot. Trust the numbers, not your eyes. Eventually your brain will begin to recognize certain angles regardless of the odd perceptions.

This first example is a 1/2 ball shot. The object ball position value is **80**. Anywhere along the diagonal "80" line would be considered 80. The natural line from the cue ball to the object ball leads to an alignment value of **40** on the side rail. The ratio is 1/2, indicating a standard 1/2 ball shot to the corner pocket.

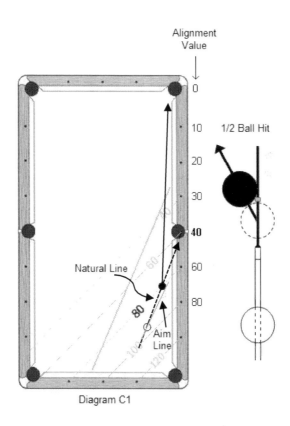

Diagram C1

Practice this shot from various object ball placements along the 80 diagonal. Place the cue ball on a natural line that would allow you to shoot the object ball straight into the imaginary diamond at the side pocket (an alignment value of 40). Each shot will require a 1/2 ball aim to send the object ball to the far corner pocket.

When you get a good feel for pocketing 1/2 ball shots where the object ball is positioned on 80, start placing the cue ball in positions to give alignment values greater than or less than 40. These shots will either be thinner or thicker than a 1/2 ball shot.

Break the shots down into quarter increments by dividing the object ball position value in half, then divide in half again. With a position value 80, half is 40, and then half again is 20. So our basic aim points are now broken down into quarter increments of 20. An alignment value of 0 is straight in, 20 would be a 3/4 ball hit, 40 a 1/2 ball hit, and 60 a 1/4 ball hit.

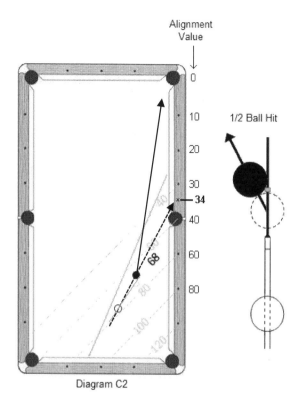

Diagram C2

This is another 1/2 ball shot from Zone C. Stand at the end rail near the lower left corner pocket and visualize the object ball position lines running diagonally. We see that the object ball is almost halfway between the 60 and 80, not quite 70, so a position value of **68** looks good. The natural line points to an alignment value around **34**, which gives a shot ratio of 1/2, indicating a 1/2 ball hit is required to pocket the ball in the far corner pocket.

The more you work with this system, the better you'll get at recognizing the various fractional hits. You'll also begin to notice just how often the 1/2 ball shot comes up. It is very common. This is why it is important to view each shot from the 1/2 ball perspective, to get an idea whether the shot is thinner, thicker, or dead on a 1/2 ball aim.

The object ball in this example has a position value of **80**. By dividing 80 in half to get 40, then 40 in half to get 20, we find that our basic aim points are in increments of 20. An alignment value of 20 would be a 3/4 hit, 40 would be a 1/2, and 60 a 1/4. Since our natural line in this shot points straight to an alignment value of **60**, we would use a 1/4 ball aim to cut this into the far corner pocket.

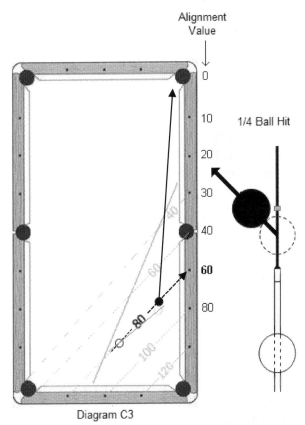

Diagram C3

Be sure to use medium cue ball speed, hitting just above center. We want the cue ball to roll into the object ball rather than slide into it. If the balls are old and dull (dirty), there will be more friction between the balls when they hit, which will create more throw than normal. This is collision-induced throw, and it can thicken the shot up by another 2 or 3 degrees if the conditions are right for it.

When it comes to collision-induced throw, it's good to know that a softer stroke on thinner shots increases the amount of throw that takes place. When the object ball is far from the pocket, an extra couple of degrees in throw could easily result in missing the pocket by a few inches. This is where you must pay attention to what is happening. Sometimes you'll need to adjust for certain conditions, while other times you won't. The best way to learn this is to pay close attention to what you are doing, and then pay attention to the results.

Remember that collision-induced throw is typically more extreme on thicker hits than thinner hits. However, speed is a factor also. Shooting a thin cut shot (a 1/4 ball or thinner) slowly will have more throw than if you put a little more steam behind it. Shooting a thicker cut shot (a 1/2 ball or thicker) firm, like a stun shot with no spin, will have more throw than if you hit it with a medium speed and rolling cue ball. That's why it's important to get a feel for speed on certain shots. Using a good medium speed works for about everything.

The maximum amount of throw occurs on stun shots around 5/8 to a 1/2 ball hit. It can be nearly 5 degrees, plenty enough to cause the object ball to miss the pocket by several inches! So, when these shot angles come up, and you have to shoot firm in order to gain position on the next shot or to avoid possible trouble, there are things you can do to help reduce the excess throw. Outside english allows the cue ball to roll off the object ball, reducing some of the collision-induced throw. Using top or bottom spin can also greatly reduce the amount of throw that occurs.

Short of these options, the only other way to deal with excessive throw is to aim the shot a little thinner, just a tiny fraction thinner, probably a millimeter or two thinner than the cut requires. This is the trickiest option because it requires an experienced feel to know exactly how much to compensate based on the speed you intend to use.

Here we have another 1/2 ball shot. Similar to a previous example (Diagram C1), the object ball position is **80** and the alignment value is **40**. The only difference is that both the cue ball and the object ball are farther away from the side rail, making the angle look different than the angle in Diagram C1. But anywhere along the 80 line is considered 80, so the shots are the same, regardless of how they look to your eyes.

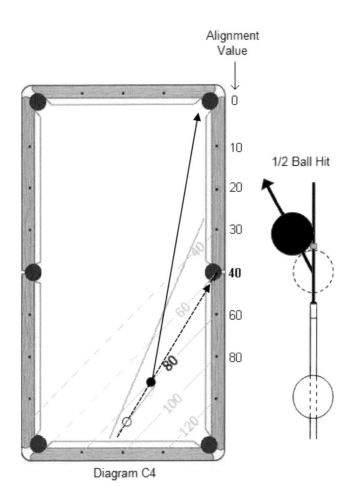

Diagram C4

Let's look at two more Zone C shots. This object ball is resting at a position of about **74**. The natural line points to an alignment value near **28**. We divide 74 in half and find the 1/2 ball shot alignment, which is 37. Dividing 37 in half gets our quarter increment values, which would be around 18, making an alignment of 18 a 3/4 ball shot, 37 a 1/2 ball shot, and 55 a 1/4 ball shot. With an actual alignment of **28**, this shot lies in-between a 3/4 ball hit and a 1/2 ball hit, making it a **5/8**. So we aim for the 5/8 ball aim point and back-cut the ball into the pocket.

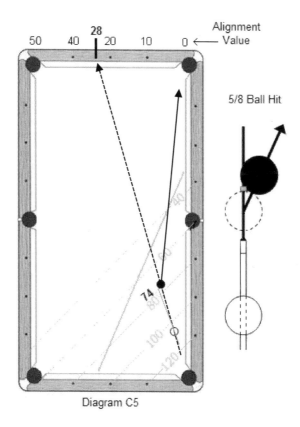

Diagram C5

Remember to pay attention to speed and roll. You want the cue ball rolling into the object ball. At this angle a sliding cue ball (stun shot) will increase the collision-induced throw dramatically. Instead of a

65

normal amount of throw (a couple of degrees), we'll get a good 4 or 5 degrees, causing the ball to hit the end rail way left of our targeted pocket. We don't want this! The system is designed to incorporate a normal amount of throw for every shot using a standard medium speed. It's worth repeating that if a firmer speed is needed, you should use top spin, draw, or outside english to reduce unwanted throw. If you elect to use english, it won't take much, and using too much could spell disaster. When the object ball is far from the pocket, like in the previous shot, using english requires an experienced feel.

This is the second time I've mentioned "experienced feel" when it comes to pocketing certain shots. This is not quite the same *feel* we are working on as far as become a player that can just "see the shots." The experience and feel required for spinning balls in and dealing with collision-induced throw is a finer aspect of the game. You'll begin to develop this as you become a more consistent shot maker.

Look at it like this: Becoming a feel player, the player that simply steps up and sees the shot, is like learning how to tune a guitar. Once you become fluent in the standard tuning process, you will automatically begin fine-tuning each string as needed because your brain will be more equipped to recognize the little subtle changes needed in tone or pitch. Of course, if you're tone-deaf, you may want to ignore this analogy. Nevertheless, when it comes to playing pool, the same fine-tunings are taking place within your brain. Just be patient and pay attention to what you are doing and what is happening in return.

Our last Zone C shot is another back-cut to the right corner. The object ball has a position value of **88**, and our natural/alignment line provides us with a value near **65**. Quickly, we think like this: Half of 88 is 44, and half of 44 is 22. We have quarter increments of 22. So an alignment value of 22 would be a 3/4 ball shot, 44 a 1/2 ball shot, and 66 a 1/4 ball shot. An alignment value of **65** is close enough to the 1/4 ball alignment (66) that we can use a 1/4 ball aim.

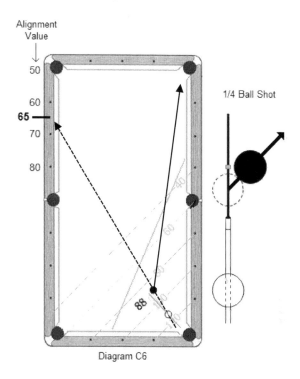

Diagram C6

Make it a point to practice the examples given, and also setup your own shots. The more you work within a particular zone, the quicker you'll master every shot in that zone.

Now let's move onto pocketing balls into the side pockets...

Side Pocket Aiming Zone

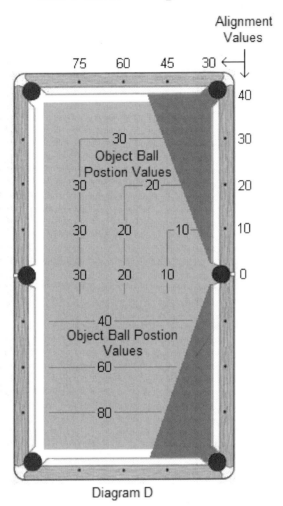

Diagram D

The right side pocket is our targeted pocket. Object ball position values are shown in the gray shaded area. There are two ranges of values we will be using, based on the natural/alignment line of the shot. As we did with zones A, B and C, you should try to memorize this diagram.

The alignment values on the end rail (from 30 to 75) will only be used for object balls positioned in the 40 to 80 range. The alignment values on the side rail are used for object balls located in either range (10 to 30, or 40 to 80) depending on the shot. This will make more sense very soon.

NOTE: Notice how the 10 to 30 position lines extend beyond the side pockets, crossing the center of the table. A ball sitting on the center line between the side pockets, or even a few inches beyond the center line, is still considered to be in the 10 to 30 position range. Determining which position numbers to use depends on where the alignment line leads. This will become clearer with the following examples.

The shot below has an object ball position value of **40**. The natural line points to an alignment value of **20** on the side rail. A simple 1/2 ball hit will send this object ball into the right side pocket.

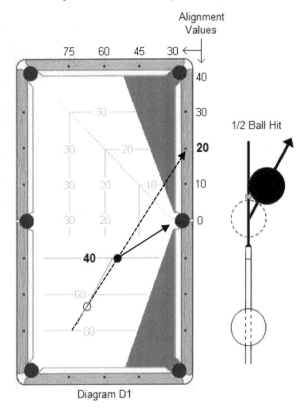

Diagram D1

Any time the alignment line leads to a rail on the opposite side/half of the table from where the object ball is resting, we consider the object ball to be in the 40 to 80 position range. If the line leads to a rail on the same side/half of the table where the object ball is resting, we'll use the 10 to 30 position range to determine a position value for the ball. In this example the alignment line crosses to the other half of the table from where the object ball is positioned. So we use the 40 to 80 range to assign a position value to the ball.

When we are using the 40 to 80 range, halfway between the center line of the table and the 40 line would be 30.

It is important to remember that a ball sitting on the center line of the table (from side pocket to side pocket) is always considered to be in the 10 to 30 position value range.

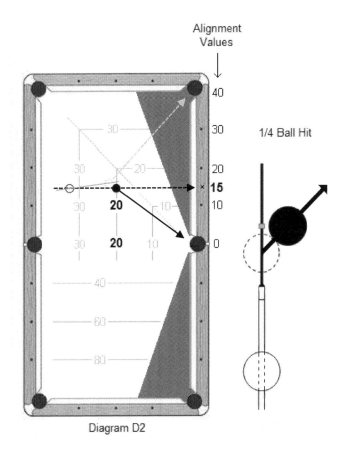

Alignment
Values

40

30   1/4 Ball Hit

20

15

10

20

20   0

Diagram D2

In the shot above, the natural line points to an alignment value of **15** on the side the rail. Since the natural line points to a rail on the same side of the table where the object ball is resting, the object ball position is considered to be in the 10 to 30 range. Applying our 10 to 30 position values, we easily see that this object ball is on **20**. This gives us an overhang of 15/20 (or 3/4), so 1/4 must overlap. Aiming at the left **1/4** aim point will send the ball into the sidepocket. And be sure to use a rolling cue ball speed or you'll slide along the tangent line and scratch in the corner, as shown with the gray line.

Here we have the natural line pointing to an alignment value of **30** on the end rail. Since the line is pointing toward a rail on the opposite side of the table from where the object ball is resting, we consider the object ball to be in the 40 to 80 range. Apply the 40 to 80 position values and we find the ball to be sitting on **60**, making this a simple 1/2 ball shot.

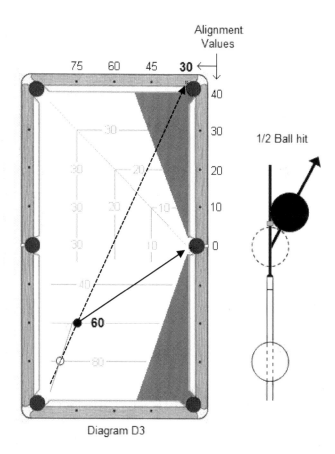

Diagram D3

NOTE: Anytime the object ball is positioned on 60, and the alignment value is anywhere between 30 on the side rail and 30 on the end rail, a 1/2 ball aim will send the ball into the side pocket, even if the alignment value is 40 on the side rail. This works due to the margin of error at the side pocket. It's like this: An alignment of 40 would give us a 40/60 overhang ratio, which is 2/3, and our overlap would be 1/3, indicating an exact 1/3 aim point is needed. We don't have to be that exact. Sure, a 1/3 aim will send the ball closer to center pocket, but a 1/2 ball aim would simply send the ball about one inch left of center pocket. It still hits the pocket! Try it for yourself.

This concludes the various zones used for pocketing cut shots. The more you practice, the more consistent you'll become. And remember that this book is geared toward helping you develop a feel for pocketing balls, so that eventually you'll be the type of player that just "sees the shots."

Applying English

English can be a fantastic tool when used appropriately. It can make for a beautiful shot or create a very ugly one. The most common mistake most players make is using too much english. Often we apply more spin than needed, or we apply spin when none is needed. If you know your cue stick well enough to be able to dance the cue ball around the table with various spins, avoiding trouble and misses, then you can skip this section. For those of you that struggle with shots that require english, or insist on using english on shots that don't need it, only to end up missing balls, you may want to read on.

Most cue sticks play differently when applying english. The shaft deflects and the cue ball squirts off line. We're not going to explore the exact physics of why this happens, but I will provide a basic explanation. The most important thing to know about deflection/squirt is how to compensate for it, but understanding why it happens can have benefits also. Knowledge builds confidence.

When the tip of a 19-ounce cue stick strikes the center of a cue ball, which weighs 6 ounces, the cue stick absorbs the full force of the ball (the 6 ounces pushes back). Since the cue stick is more than three times the weight of the cue ball, it continues moving straight forward, forcing the cue ball to be sent away in the same direction as the stroke. The weight of the cue stick and the weight of the ball are on the same path. One is heavier than the other, so the lighter one gets pushed on down the path. This is obvious, of course, because you can see it happen.

This is what you don't see happening: The shaft of a pool cue typically weighs only 4 to 5 ounces. When the shaft collides with the heavier 6-ounce ball, it immediately feels the force of the heavier ball. At the same time, the weight of the rest of the cue (the butt end) rushes in, backing up the shaft and forcing the cue ball away. The shaft is caught in the middle, sandwiched between the full weight of the cue ball and the weight of the rest of the cue stick. It can't escape the forces on either end of the collision and must absorb the full force of impact. The tip of the cue takes the most abuse, which causes it to mushroom out after enough forceful impacts. Since all the forces are aligned on the same path (the stroke line, or line of aim), there is no deflection. Like a large truck rear-ending a small car, the cue stick simply pushes its weight on down the path while the cue ball hopelessly tries to push back.

When the cue tip strikes the cue ball off-center, left or right, there are two paths available for the opposing forces. The larger force (the weight of the cue stick) travels down the stroke path, while the weight of the cue ball pushes back against the tip of the shaft at an angle away from the stroke path. Since the tip isn't hitting the center of the ball, the cue shaft is no longer sandwiched between the full weight of the ball and the heavy butt end of the cue stick. As the tip strikes the side of the ball, the light shaft feels the 6-ounce weight of the ball pushing it away from the stroke path. The weight of the rest of the cue stick rushes in and forces the shaft even farther from the path, deflecting the cue tip away from the cue ball as the ball begins to spin away. This is not something you can watch with your eyes. It happens instantaneously.

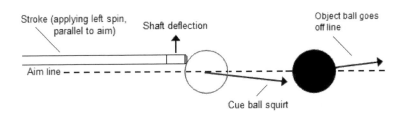

The cue ball, being a round object hit on one side or the other, will squirt in the opposite direction of the hit every time, regardless of deflection. More deflection causes less cue ball squirt, and less deflection causes more cue ball squirt. There are things we do to help minimize deflection, like using chalk to keep the tip from slipping off the side of the ball. (A miscue is a prime example of maximum deflection because the weight of the ball pushes the shaft completely off its path.) Cue manufacturers today are getting better at designing low-deflection shafts, which should really be called "low-squirt" shafts. This is done by making the last few inches of the shaft lighter, which increases shaft deflection, thereby reducing cue ball squirt.

Before the invention of low-deflection shafts, players would simply compensate their aiming to account for cue ball squirt. Many players prefer this over investing in a low-deflection shaft. There is much to be said about the feel of a cue, developing a touch for knowing exactly how much to compensate on any given shot. The choice is yours.

So how do we compensate our aim when applying english? The most widely used method is the "pivot" method. Some actually call it the *secret* to using english. The following illustrations show how it works. First we cue the shot up with a center cue ball hit along the aim line.

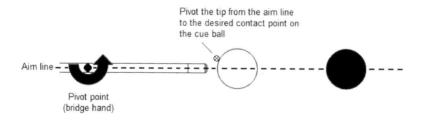

Now simply keep your bridge hand in place and pivot the butt end of the cue just enough to align the cue tip with the contact point for your desired english. Stroke the shot from there. Doing this pivot move actually changes your aim line. It looks like there's no way the cue ball will go where it should. But when the inevitable deflection and squirt happens, the cue ball will squirt right back onto the original aim line. It will also have your applied spin on it.

Many players do this automatically. Instead of doing the pivot move, they automatically approach the shot with their body and stroke aligned for the compensated aim. If you can do this, great! If not, just pivot your cue as needed.

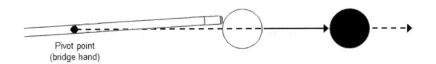

Pivot point
(bridge hand)

That's it! Now you know how to compensate when using english. However, the smartest thing any player can do is minimize how much and how often english gets used. You'll find consistency easier to obtain by incorporating natural position for most shots, using only follow and draw. Side spin is a special tool that should be reserved for shots where it is really needed, like glitter on artwork.

Note that all cue shafts are not equal. Due to wood grain, ferrule material, and tip hardness, the pivot point will not be in the same location for every cue. Usually, a standard bridge of about 8 to 10 inches will provide an accurate pivot point. Some cues, however, due to having more deflection, may require a shorter bridge for a pivot point. You'll have to experiment with your particular cue to find its magic spot. You may find that you only need to compensate your aim when using inside english, while outside english allows you to shoot directly at the aim point while applying english at the same time.

Never use english just for the sake of using it. If you don't need it, don't use it. If you do need it, usually no more than 1 tip from center is all you'll need. You'll find that 1/2 a tip of english will handle most position shots when needed. A ½ tip of english is simply when the edge of your cue tip is flush with the center of the cue ball. A 1/2 tip of left spin would have the right side of your tip lined to center cue ball. A 1/2 tip of draw would require the top side of your tip to be flush with the center of the cue ball. There are many combinations, such as top-left, bottom-right, etc...all of which can easily be gauged with the tip in reference to center cue ball.

Don't forget to chalk! A great habit to develop is to chalk the cue tip before each shot. And don't chalk it like your cue tip is a drill bit trying to bore a hole through the chalk. Brush the chalk over the sides of your tip. The chalk will last longer and miscues will be a thing of the past. It does no good to know what needs to happen, and to know how to make it happen, only to stroke the shot and hear that horrible click-sound. Don't be that person.

Banking

This section of Poolology is geared to improving your bank shots. We are not going to dive into a full-blown banking course. Remember, Poolology is about aiming, so we are going to focus on aiming bank shots, learning how to use fractional ball aiming as a tool for banking.

There are several methods available for evaluating banks. In this brief banking section, we are going to use the most effective and simplest of these methods: The "Split the Difference" method.

First things first...unless you are playing one-pocket or bank pool, electing to shoot a bank shot over a cut shot is not a good idea. That easy straight bank to hold position for the next shot, for instance, could hit a dead spot in the cushion, causing you to miss the bank and lose the game. A good rule to follow: **Never bank a ball you can cut.** With that said, there are times you'll have to shoot a bank shot. In these situations it's nice to have confidence in knowing what you are doing.

Before we look at any banking concepts, we should review three basic principles for banking, things that you must know and understand in order to be a proficient banker. No handy banking system would be very handy without properly understanding the basics.

Principle #1: The Angle

Generally, a ball rolling into a cushion will bounce away at an angle fairly equal to the approach angle. In other words: **Angle in = Angle out**. The technical term for the approach angle is *angle of incidence*. The bounce away (rebound) is called the *angle of reflection*. We don't have to be technical in order to understand the concept, so we'll use the terms **angle in** and **angle out**.

Principle #2: Shot Speed

Usually, shooting hard decreases the rebound angle off the cushion. When the cue ball or object ball hits a cushion, the cushion caves in a bit. The ball actually buries into the cushion and then gets pushed out. A hard-struck ball buries deeper, causing the rebounded *angle out* to be narrower than the *angle in*. You can say it "tightens up" the bank, or "straightens it out", which is fine if that's your intention for the shot. But if you expect a dead/straight bank, where the angle in equals the angle out, you'll be disappointed when you slam it and the ball hits short of the intended pocket. If you have to shoot the bank forcefully, and you are not trying to tighten it up, use about 1/2 a tip of **outside english** to counter the shortening action caused by the cushion. The diagram below illustrates this principle.

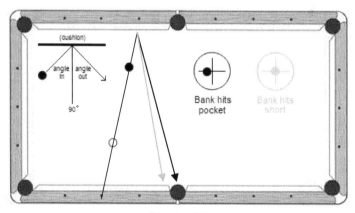

Diagram E1

The black line in Diagram E1 represents a dead (lined up) bank, *angle in* equals *angle out*. The gray line indicates where the object ball will hit if we shoot hard with center ball, no english. A medium to soft stroke with center ball would pocket the shot easily. However, it is usually not desirable to shoot bank shots softly. Too often the table/cloth condition will cause a soft-struck ball to roll off line. To avoid this, most banks should be shot with a good medium speed using

81

a touch of outside spin to counter any narrowing effect caused by the cushion.

Using a half tip of outside (left) english with a medium stroke would bank this ball into the side pocket. The left spin causes the object ball to spin to the right off the cushion, which sends it toward the intended pocket. The harder you hit the shot the more english you may need to use in order to compensate for the cushion action. It really depends on the table. This is where experience comes into play.

Principle #3: Cue ball Spin

As shown above, english is an important factor when it comes to pocketing bank shots. Using outside english (left in the previous example, Diagram E1) will cause the object ball to spin to the right coming off the cushion, widening the rebound angle. Using inside english (right spin in this case) will cause the object ball to spin left, shortening the rebound angle. Remember, hitting this particular shot firm with center ball will shorten up the shot anyway, sending the object ball along the gray line. If we were to use inside english (right spin), we could shorten the rebound angle even more, which would not be needed for this shot. The example on the next page demonstrates when inside english would possibly be needed.

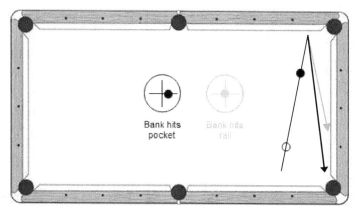

Diagram E2

Here the dead bank lands nearly a diamond short of the pocket (gray line). Shooting straight, very firm, with center ball or a draw stroke could possibly tighten the shot up enough to make it. However, using inside english will allow the shot to be made without having to slam the ball. Apply a little inside (right spin) as shown, and use medium to firm speed. Shooting the shot too hard could actually tighten it up so much that the ball hits above the intended pocket.

As you can see, speed and spin are crucial factors on most bank shots. It is something that must be learned through experience. When a player has a "feel" for bank shots, it means he or she not only knows where to hit the cushion in order to make the ball, but also knows exactly how hard or how soft to hit the shot – using just the right amount of spin if needed – to make it all work.

The next few pages illustrate the quickest and easiest way to find the correct angle for any bank shot. We will be using the split-the-difference method, counting the diamonds to pinpoint the appropriate aim spot on the rail. I've found that many players do not know or understand how to do this. It really is the simplest method to use.

Once you are able to locate the appropriate bank spot on the rail, the Poolology aiming system can then be used to drill that bank shot right into the pocket. This neat little trick utilizes position values from Zone B. But first we need to learn how to find that bank spot, so here we go!

Diagram E3

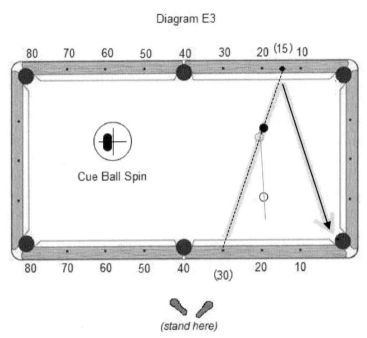

Cue Ball Spin

(stand here)

Label the diamonds as shown, starting with zero at the intended pocket end of the table. To locate the bank spot on the opposite rail, stand as shown above. Ignore the cue ball. Hold your cue stick over the object ball with the tip pointing toward the opposite rail (you can actually rest the cue tip on the cushion of the rail) and hold the butt end/wrap over the rail directly in front of you. Now simply find a line directly over the object ball that points your cue tip to a diamond value on the opposite rail that equals half the diamond value below the wrap or butt end of your cue stick where you're standing.

Here, with our cue shaft directly above the center of the object ball

84

and the tip resting on the cushion of the far rail, we find the natural bank line. The cue tip points to a diamond value of 15, while the butt end or wrap of the cue hovers over a value of 30.   This spot on the rail (15) is our target. We have "split the difference". If the cue ball happened to be on this line, it would be a straight-in bank shot. Here, based on where the cue ball is located, we need a fractional hit to send the object ball toward 15.

Are you with me so far? We have a bank spot of 15 on the far rail. We are not straight in. We'll have to cut the object ball toward our bank spot. So what fractional hit is needed to do this? Well, this is where the trick comes in...

We are going to treat this bank shot like a regular cut shot. But instead of cutting the ball into a targeted pocket, we'll be cutting it into the bank spot on the rail. If we view our bank spot as a targeted pocket, we can apply the aiming system and easily determine the required fractional hit that would send the object ball to that spot.

The following diagrams illustrate the trick. If we imagine moving the end rail up to our targeted bank spot (Diagram E4), the bank becomes a simple Zone B cut shot (DiagramE5).

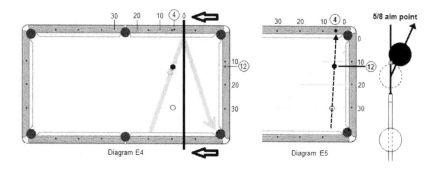

With our bank spot visualized as a targeted corner pocket, the spot becomes our zero point. From there we add alignment values up the rail, one diamond distance away would be 10, two diamonds would be

20, and so on... Note that these alignment values will not necessarily correspond to any actual diamond/marker locations, as shown in Diagram E4, but the diamonds can still be used to help determine the location of our alignment values.

Now apply the Zone B object ball position values to the end rail. Remember, in Zone B the diamond closest to the targeted pocket indicates an object ball position line of 10, the next diamond is 20, then 30. With the position values added, we see that the object ball position here is **12**.

The natural line (from the center of the cue ball through the center of the object ball) points to an alignment value of **4**. If we had an alignment value of 6 this would be a half-ball shot. (Remember how to find our quarter increments? 12 divided by two is 6, then 6 divided by two is 3. A value of 3 would be a 3/4 shot, 6 is 1/2, and 9 would be 1/4.) Our alignment value is 4, which is between a 3/4 hit and a 1/2 ball hit. We could use the **5/8** aim point for this shot. See "In-between Aim Points". Due to friction between the cue ball and the object ball upon impact, outside spin (left english here) should be used when shooting this shot to minimize throw.

This next example may appear confusing at first. However, we are doing the trick in the same manner as the previous example. First we locate the bank line, which we find to be from 52 to 26 as shown. Next we make the bank spot on the rail (26) our target and assign it a value of zero. Then we add our alignment scale values from there, beginning one diamond distance from zero. The first value will be 10, then 20, etc... Now we assign a position value to the object ball. (use Zone B object ball position values) Remember, zero begins at the target. Here the target is a spot on the rail. If we could move the end rail up to this spot, we'd see that the object ball is fully in Zone B at a position of **20**. The natural line points to an alignment value of **10** on the targeted rail. This is a ratio of 1/2, which means it is a half-ball shot.

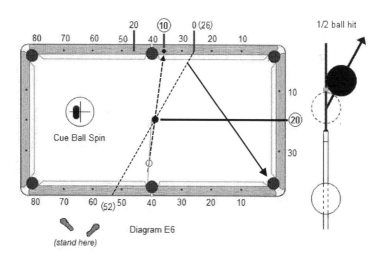

Diagram E6

Outside english should be used to offset any frictional throw or collision-induced spin caused by the cueball striking the object ball. Anytime the cue ball is not making a full hit with the object ball, a certain amount of throw and collision-induced spin occurs. If you are cutting a ball to the right, and the cue ball strikes the left side of the object ball, there is just enough friction at the point of impact to cause the object ball to be pushed offline a bit (throw). This friction also imparts a small spin on the object ball (collision-induced spin).

Here we have another 1/2 ball bank shot. The bank line is visualized as shown from 14 to 7. We make that spot on the bank rail (7) our target and give it an alignment value of zero. One diamond distance up the rail from there we'll call 10, then 20, etc... This is our alignment scale. If we follow the natural line from the cue ball through the object ball, it leads to an alignment value of 15 on the scale. Now we apply the Zone B position values for the shot and find that this object ball is positioned at **30**. With an alignment value of **15** and the object ball resting on 30, we get a ratio of **1/2**, making this a simple half-ball shot.

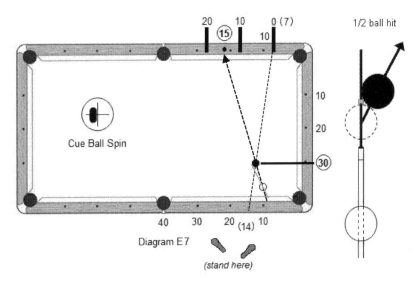

Diagram E7

(stand here)

Once again, taking into consideration the effects of friction, we'll use outside english for the shot. Be sure to follow through completely. Stroke the shot with confidence using medium speed. Often the speed is determined by position play, or strategy, depending on the specific game you are playing.

Full-table banks can be figured the same way, only instead of using Zone B values for object ball positions we'll use Zone A.

Diagram E8

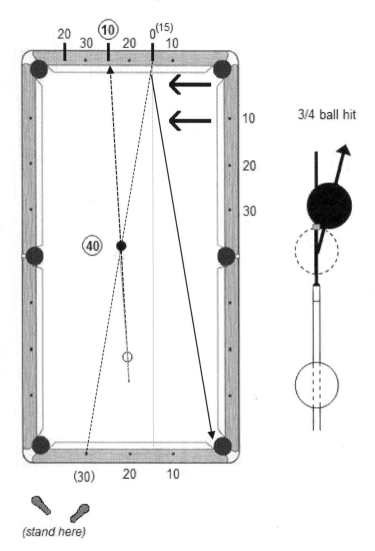

3/4 ball hit

(stand here)

For this shot we find our bank line to be from 30 to 15. So we imagine that spot (15) as our targeted pocket, like sliding that right corner pocket over to that spot, making it zero. Then we add alignment values on across the rail – one diamond distance left from 0 is 10, then

89

20, etc... Next, determine the object ball position using the Zone A position value lines. This ball has a position value near **40**. Center-to-center leads us to an alignment value of **10** on the far rail, indicating the shot requires a 1/4 overhang, which means a **3/4** overlap/fractional hit is needed to send the ball to our target spot.

With so many variables affecting the outcome of a bank shot, approximations are often par for the course. Experience will help you fine tune the little things needed to make it all work.

Practice visualizing bank shots in this manner and you'll begin to develop a natural eye for determining which fractional hit is needed to pocket about any bank. Remember, if you are cutting a ball backward toward the bank spot, you should apply outside spin to counter any frictional effect between the balls when they collide. Don't overdo it! A little spin can go a long way, but a lot of spin can go the wrong way!

How it All Works

Two mathematical components were merged to develop the Poolology system. The images on this page provide a brief explanation of that development.

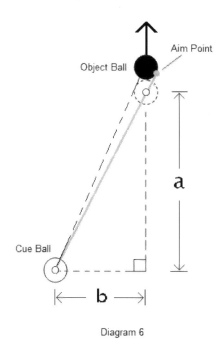

Diagram 6

The image on the left shows the geometry used for determining fractional hits.

The arrow is pointing toward the pocket, the ratio **b/a** indicates the fractional hit needed to send the object ball in this direction. Here the b/a ration is 1/2, which means a half-ball fractional hit will send the object ball along the arrow.

This is standard fractional ball knowledge and has been around for decades. Alone it doesn't do us much good. Determining accurate values for the ratio is guesswork, which is why traditional fractional ball aiming falls short of being a great learning tool.

This particular component is embedded into the Poolology aiming system. It provides *Alignment Values* for given shots. The second component looks a bit more artistic, as you can see on the following page. It provides *Object Ball Position Values*, a new concept that takes fractional ball aiming to a new level.

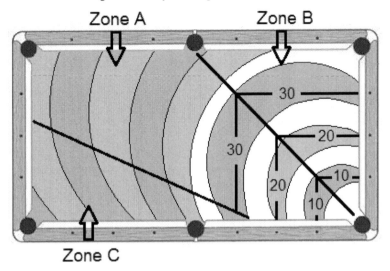

Zone A   Zone B

Zone C

The crescent-shaped areas in the table above show the original algebraic concept for the Poolology system. Using the standard formula for a circle, $(x-h)^2 + (y-k)^2 = r^2$, where h and k and r are all equal to the radius of our circle, and also equal diamond distances from the pocket.

Each crescent was plotted using this formula. Plotting the 20 crescent, for instance, looks like this: $(x-10)^2 + (y-10)^2 = 100$. The diameter of our circle is two diamonds, which we are calling 20. We only plot the points within the playing surface of the table, which gives us a partial circular pattern as shown in the diagram.

Now here comes the fascinating part... If we place an object ball anywhere along the circumference of this circle (anywhere along the circumference is considered a position of 20), and we draw a line from the center of the ball to the center opening of the corner pocket (also located on the circumference of our circle at a position we are calling 0), then draw another line from the center of the ball to the first diamond (which we are calling 10), we create an inscribed angle within the circle/crescent.

The two lines inscribing our angle are called chords. The chord that has its endpoint at the pocket is our shot line for the ball. The chord with its endpoint at the first diamond is our alignment line, also called the *natural line* or *alignment line* throughout this book. The image on the left shows the inscribed angle created, which ends up being 28 degrees. It is found by using the **Inscribed Angle Theorem** and doing some fancy calculations using similar triangles and a central angle that shares the same arc and endpoints belonging to our inscribed angle.

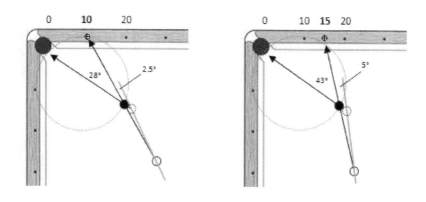

When the cue ball leaves the alignment line for our aim line, we have an offset angle that gets added to this 28 degrees. The offset here is about 2.5 degrees, which brings our shot angle very close to a 30-degree 1/2 ball fractional hit. The image on the right shows how the 1/4 ball shot works from this same distance. Our alignment line points to 15. The inscribed angle turns out to be around 43 degrees. Adding the 5-degree offset brings the shot to 48 degrees, which is a 1/4 ball fractional shot.

As exciting and fun as all of this is, I hope I don't disappoint you by not digging deeper into the actual calculations. After all, this is not a geometry lesson. Knowing how to do the math has nothing to do with knowing how to aim the shots.   Let's move on...

If we move the object ball to any spot along the circumference of our circle and draw the appropriate chords again (in either of the images above) the inscribed angle remains the same. The Poolology system uses this inscribed angle method, along with the offset angle, to determine the appropriate aim point for any given shot. The offset angle is normally between 1 and 5 degrees, depending on the distance between the balls and the degree of the cut. Thinner cuts have higher offsets. We'll look at this offset angle in a moment.

All of this sounds a bit confusing, huh? Fortunately, the original concept of circular/crescent shapes can be simplified. By linearizing the crescent areas (straight-lining the heart of each crescent, as shown in the original concept image with black lines at 10, 20 and 30) we simplify the process without comprising too much on accuracy, making the system more user-friendly. Instead of dealing with a table of imaginary circles that often don't correspond to the diamonds, we now have three straight-lined zones for corner pocket shots. The side pocket zone was created in the same manner, first with circles/crescents then simplified with straight lines.

A fair amount of experimentation was used to help determine exact alignment values that could be used in conjunction with the position values. These alignment values account for a typical amount of collision-induced throw, which is why a rolling cue ball speed is an important factor.

The Poolology aiming system works very accurately as long as the distance between the cue ball and object ball is greater than about 8 inches. This is where the offset angle comes into play. When the distance is closer than 8 inches, the offset angle is greater than 4 degrees, which causes the shot line to shift too far from the pocket. A larger shift creates a missed shot, so a thinner aim point is needed to correct this. The following diagrams illustrate the effects of distance v/s offset angles.

With both balls positioned on the natural alignment line (center to center), the offset angle is measured from the alignment line to the actual aim line. As the distance between the cue ball and object ball decreases, the offset angle increases, and vice versa.

The system is targeting a near center-pocket shot most of the time, meaning the alignment values and position values provide a fractional hit to send the object ball toward the center of the pocket. I say "most of the time" because there are shots where the ball is being targeted left or right of center-pocket. Remember, we are using the entire pocket, accounting for collision-induced throw and an allowable margin of error at the pocket. The most throw occurs for cut angles between a 3/8 fractional hit and a 5/8 hit. The margin of error at the pocket increases as the distance between the object ball and pocket decreases. What the offset angle does is shift the actual shot angle a bit left or right of the shot line approaching the pocket. The shot angle does not change – it shifts.

Let's say we are shooting a 1/2 ball shot to the right, as shown above. When the distance between the cue ball and object ball decreases, the offset angle increases, shifting the entire 30-degree shot to the left. This shift, measured in degrees, is equal to the offset angle. From cue ball #1 (a 5-foot distance) the offset angle is about 1 degree. From cue ball #2 (a 1-foot distance) the offset is bordering 3 degrees. The difference between the two offset angles is less than 2 degrees. From within this 2-degree window is where the system is targeting the shot. Shooting from cue ball #1 will result in a less than 2-degree angle difference at the pocket, compared to shooting from cue ball #2. This is not enough to cause a miss. Here is why...

With the cue ball 5 feet from the object ball, the maximum distance between the ball and the pocket must be less than about 2 feet on a 7ft table and 4 feet on a 9ft table. The margin of error at the pocket is wider than the total amount of shift caused by the offset angle. There are exceptions of course, like when the pockets are super-tight or the table is a 10 or 12-footer. If that's the case, longer shots would need to be fine-tuned by aiming a touch thicker than the system indicates, maybe a 1/16 of a ball thicker. This adjustment is rarely needed. It's the close-up shots, as shown above with cue ball #3, that we need adjustments because the offset angle is very high from here, around 10 degrees or higher, which almost equates to an entire quarter aim point. At 6 to 8 inches, we need to aim one eighth of a ball thinner, and closer than 6 inches we need to aim a whole quarter-ball thinner.

Each cut angle produces different offset angles in accordance with the distance between the balls. Our first example was a standard 30-degree cut shot, a 1/2 ball shot. The next couple of illustrations show the offset angles for 3/4 and a 1/4 ball shots. Notice how the changing offset for the 3/4 ball hit below results in very little angle shift toward the targeted pocket. Shots at this angle would need very little adjustment, if any at all. Aim for the 3/4 ball aim point and send the ball to the pocket.

Cue Ball #1   Cue Ball #2   Cue Ball #3

With the 1/4 ball shot, as with the 1/2 ball, the offset angle dramatically increases as the cue ball gets closer than about 8 inches from the object ball. A thinner aim point is needed to compensate for this. However, the difference between the offset angle at cue ball #1 and the offset at cue ball #2 is within a reasonable tolerance (less than 2 degrees). So there is no need to make adjustments for the longer distance shots, other than for super-tight pockets or extra large tables, as described earlier. Here are the offsets for varying distances on a 1/4 ballshot...

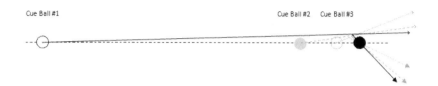

The change in perspective between the cue ball and object ball also changes as the distance changes. So even though we keep the same aim point for the varying distances, we are not really aiming at the exact same place on the object ball. The aim point shifts slightly as our view of the object ball shifts. It all works out quite conveniently.

Taking all of this into account, the Poolology aiming system has proven to be a very nice enhancement for traditional fractional-ball aiming. Much of the guesswork has been eliminated, leaving you – the player – a better opportunity to quickly develop a feel for aiming.

Practice

Simply throwing a handful of balls out on the table and shooting them into the pockets, regardless of how many hours you spend doing this, is not an effective means of practice. I know what you're thinking...*But isn't it still practice?* The answer is no, not really. Instead of working on areas of your game that need improvement, you are reinforcing any flaws or bad habits you may have.

If you insist on randomly shooting balls and calling it practice, then do yourself a favor and record your "practice" sessions on video, or take detailed notes of the shots you miss, bad position plays, etc... Afterwards, watch the video or study your notes and look for patterns of consistent error. You may find that most of the missed shots were thin 1/4 ball cuts to the left, or long shots across the center of the table. This will highlight your weaknesses, your limitations, and then you'll know what needs practiced. Understanding and acknowledging your weaknesses is a very important step to playing better pool.

Go out to your local office supply store and purchase a package of binder-hole reinforcements, those small adhesive donuts. They come in white or multicolored options and make great ball position markers for practicing trouble shots. If you find that a certain fractional ball hit repeatedly gives you the fits, set a few of those shots up using the donut markers. Pool balls sit perfectly in the hole of the little donut. You can even use the color ones to set up a multi-ball runout, like the last four balls of a nine ball rack. Remember, practice should be fun!

With Poolology, practice is simplified to shot-making. You must be able to recognize and hit that aim spot. It's all about the aiming. Study and practice the diagrams in this book and your pocketing skills will advance to a higher level in a fraction of the time it would take using conventional practice methods. The most important thing is to become very familiar with each aiming zone. This means you should memorize the zones! And keep in mind that other aspects of the game, as discussed throughout this book, will also require attention.

Practice should always have a goal of developing good habits. Good habits are programmed into our brain by repeating them. Unfortunately, bad habits are formed the same way, and we don't want those! Just focus on what you are doing, and observe the results. Before you know it your brain will do it for you automatically. You won't have to think about overhangs or overlaps because every shot will become natural. Once this happens, once you find yourself consistently pocketing balls, your mind will be free to focus on speed, spin, and position. First, you need to master the art of aiming.

The next two pages contain a couple of practice drills. In the first drill the balls are lined across the table at the second diamond (a position of 20 in Zone A). In order to use Zone A values, the balls on the right should go into pocket "A" while the balls on the left go into pocket "B". It doesn't matter in what order you shoot the balls.

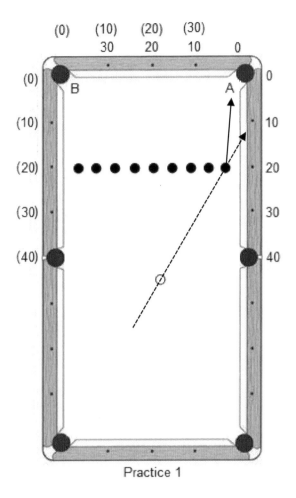

Practice 1

When shooting the balls on the right into pocket "A", each ball is resting on a position of 20, as indicated by the diamond values on the right side rail. You will use the alignment values on the end rail and the side rail to determine the appropriate fractional hit needed to pocket each ball. Start by setting up a perfect 1/2 ball shot (line the cue ball up to shoot the object ball straight into the first diamond (an alignment value of 10). It makes no difference which pocket you prefer to start with, and you can switch back and forth between shots if you'd like. But when shooting the balls on the left side of the table to pocket "B", you'll have to use the alignment values that are in parenthesis, since we'd be flipping our Zone A around to correspond to that corner pocket. This drill will help build a great feel for the various angles and fractional hits that come up within a particular zone.

This following drill should be worked in the manner as the previous, only this time the object balls are lined across at position values of 30. Set the first shot up as a half-ball hit, aiming the cue ball straight through the object ball to 15 on the rail as shown.

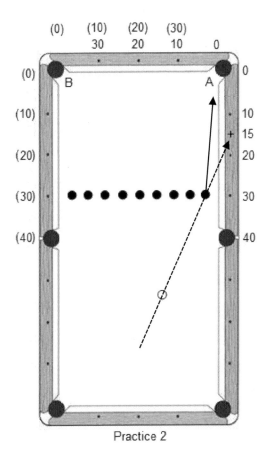

Practice 2

You can also do this same drill with the object balls lined across the table at a position value of 40. This type of practice, where the object balls are all positioned on the same value, will build a memory bank of quarter-increment scales within your brain for countless shot angles, making it possible to start automatically recognizing certain hits without even thinking about it.

The final chapter of this book, Lessons Learned, contains a sprinkle of true stories that I was fortunate enough to experience throughout my pool-playing journey. I have omitted names, with the exception of those who have passed on to the next world. I owe much of my love for this game to such players.   Enjoy....

Lessons Learned

One night, way back when I was 21 years old, I was playing pool with a friend in a bar. It was after 2:00am and the bar had already closed. My buddy was friends with the owner and he'd talked him into giving us the key to the door and the key to the pool table (a 7- foot Valley bar box) so we could have an 8-ball marathon. The marathon involved a lot of pool and a lot of drinking, and I was doing a fine job at both, drinking cherry brandy with 7-up and breaking and running racks of eight ball with ease.

My buddy was getting the worse end of it, the losing end, and he wasn't taking it well. Several times he slammed his cue stick onto the table. A few times he ran the butt-end through the sheetrock wall after racking the balls for me. I was having a great time, up by a good 15 games or so. I asked if he wanted to break. He refused, saying he'd "earn" his break and didn't need any gifts from me. I said fine and we kept playing.

A few games later, after he'd missed a ball and I ran out for the umpteenth time, he grabbed the cue ball and said, "I'm breaking, damnit!" I laughed and racked the balls. He probably hadn't broken a rack in a good hour or more. He started stroking his cue stick back and forth very quickly, saying something about showing me that he can break and run racks too, then he fired into the cue ball with everything he had.

What happened next is one of the most spectacular things I've ever witnessed on a pool table. The cue ball flew across the table in the air, just a fraction of an inch above the racked balls. It hit the cushion on the end rail at a perfect angle to come straight back across the table, where it drilled my friend right between the legs! He dropped like a sack of potatoes to the floor and I laughed so hard I thought I was going to puke up my cherry brandy. We both had tears in our eyes! I told him he'd be alright, but thirty minutes later we were at the hospital. I ended up calling someone to come and pick us up so he could have his crotch looked at by a professional. He was really hurt.

Lesson learned: Always take your time when breaking. The break shot needs to be performed with an accurate hit on the cue ball. Don't let your emotions get the better of you, because your accuracy will suffer and the balls you end up breaking just might be your own!

A few friends and I were playing a friendly nine ball ring game, $2 per ball on the 5, 7, and 9. A good old guy we called Sawdust had been getting the shaft for quite a while, not getting many opportunities. Sometimes a ring game can be brutal like that. Often, with four good players in the game, you might have to wait several racks before getting a turn at the table. And when you finally do get a turn, you'll have nothing but a kick shot, where you can't see the lowest ball and your only choice is to try and make something happen. I've seen ring games go like this five or six racks at a time. This time it was happening to Sawdust. He couldn't seem to get any opportunities, and when he did they were the type that required him to make something spectacular happen. But nothing spectacular was happening. He just kept paying out each rack, $6 every game.

After paying out for a very long time, he finally got a shot that would earn him a little cash and get him back into the game. I'd missed the five ball and left Sawdust an easy shot – the five straight in the side. With a toothpick tangling from the corner of his mouth, Sawdust grabbed his cue, strolled over to the table and said, "You sons-a-bitches are in for it now." He bent over and fired at the five with top-right english. There was a loud click and the cue ball shot sideways, away from the five ball, and scratched in the corner pocket. Sawdust flung his cue stick across the four empty tables to the right. It slammed into the far wall and bounced back and forth between a couple of metal barstools before hitting the floor.

From the corner of my eye I saw something hit the pool table near the five ball, then bobble across the table to the floor. It happened so fast that I wasn't sure what it was. Then I looked up at the face of the infamous "Badger" Trout. He was laughing uncontrollably. His mouth appeared saggy, very different looking, and then it hit me. The object that had struck the table and tumbled to the floor was his teeth, Badger's dentures.

Sawdust stormed off after his cue stick. We could hear him cursing under his breath. Badger picked his teeth up from the floor, still laughing, then rinsed them in his glass of Jim Beam and shoved them back into his mouth. It was his shot now. He shot the five in the side pocket and polished off the rest of the rack.

Lesson learned: Chalk your cue before every shot, especially if it's a money ball. And keep your teeth in your mouth at all times.

R.I.P. "Scary" Larry Mills, aka "Sawdust", and Ron "The Badger" Trout

We all miss you!

I was playing in a tournament one weekend long ago. I guess I was around 27 or 28 years old. It was a nine ball event on a Friday night, followed by eight ball on Saturday. The prior year I had won the nine ball. I received a handful of cash and a little trophy engraved with "Shenandoah Valley Nine Ball Open – First Place". This year, however, I had already lost two matches and was out of the nine ball tournament. I had done a poor job of defending my crown and figured I could make it up by gambling a little.

I started playing for drinks at first, then the money came out. I ended up winning around $400 and then lost it back, plus more. It seems that alcohol and pool are not all that compatible when you're playing $50 and $100 sets. I'd won a few sets from players that I had to spot, then the more I drank the more the spots began to kill me. Eventually I found myself playing a top-notch player. He was the official "Virginia Nine Ball Champion", having recently won the Virginia State Nine Ball Open. After a couple of sets, he told me he didn't want to take advantage of me, and said we could play sometime when I wasn't so "lit". I couldn't argue with him. By then I was getting the 7 ball and it didn't matter. There was no way I could win. Not only was he a great player, but he was a hell of a guy for not busting me when he had the chance.

After the Champ let me off the hook, I played a big fellow that agreed to spot me the 8, seeing how I was slightly over-intoxicated. I dropped my last $100. That's when I came up with what I thought was a brilliant idea to win some of my money back. I asked a friend to loan me $100. He said not if I was going to play pool with it, not tonight anyway, while I was drinking. I told him I had no intentions of playing any more pool, and he loaned me the money.

Immediately after getting this $100 I turned to the big guy that had just robbed me. He was the biggest man in the room, an overweight loudmouth with an obnoxious attitude. I said, "How about we go outside and fight for $50?" He smiled and said I was full of it. My

108

friend stood up and said he wanted his $100 back right then. I explained that all I was trying to do was win some of my money back, and that the fight would be like a boxing match – toe-to-toe, not some street fight where we slop around on the ground kicking each other in the back of the head. The big guy said no. Then an old man that was sitting near us spoke up. "If I was twenty years younger I'd take you up on that bet." I told him if he was 20 years younger he'd lose his money.

With no takers on the fight proposition, I staggered off toward my hotel room with my buddy's hundred dollars feeling very heavy in my pocket. The next day, hung over of course, I entered the eight ball tournament and lost my first match. The weekend was turning out to be a disaster. But then my friend, the one that loaned the money, took me aside and asked what the hell was wrong with me. I said, "I don't know, Badger...I guess it's just not my weekend." He shook his head in complete disappoint and said, "Don't give up, man...Just play pool." And so I did.

With my friend, the late great Badger Trout, following me to every match, I shot my way out of the loser's bracket to a 2nd place win out of a field of nearly 140 players. Badger kept a tally of break-n-runs, and said I'd run 18 racks coming out of that loser's bracket, and many more from mid-game positions. I don't remember missing a single ball.

Lesson learned: When everything seems hopeless, don't give up...just play pool. And if you love playing pool, and really want to play well, drink water instead of alcohol.

Be sure to check out the Poolology YouTube channel for the latest book updates and support videos.

Made in the USA
Middletown, DE
15 September 2018